SharePoint Calculated Columns and Validation Formulas

Everything you need to know about SharePoint formulas for SharePoint 2010 to 2019 and SharePoint Online / Office 365!

Michael T. Smith

AUTHOR

Michael T. Smith

COPYRIGHT

TRADEMARKS

Brand names, company names and product names used herein are trademarks or registered trademarks of their respective companies.

Microsmith, Inc.

ISBN 978-0-9828992-2-9

About the Author

Mike Smith is currently a Senior Instructor at MAX Technical Training in Cincinnati, Ohio. He has worn many IT hats over the last thirty years as a business owner, developer, tech writer, trainer, DBA and consultant. He is a SharePoint / Office Apps & Services MVP for 2010 - 2019 and a Microsoft Certified Trainer (MCT). He specializes in SharePoint, SQL Server, PowerShell and .NET development. Mike is a member of the Cincinnati SharePoint User Group leadership team, and when time permits, speaks at SharePoint user groups, SharePoint Saturday events and other technology events. Mike has written over 120 training and technical manuals, and now, his third SharePoint book.

You can contact the author via Twitter at @TechTrainNotes or his blog at http://TechTrainingNotes.blogspot.com.

Please post any questions, bugs, typos and suggestions to:
http://TechTrainingNotes.blogspot.com/2018/10/Sharepoint-Calculated-Columns-and.html

Acknowledgments

A book like this one owes a lot to many people. Here's just a few…

➢ My wife Kathy and my four sons - for their never-ending patience with my working way too much.
➢ Denise Bartick and the MAX Technical Training team - for giving me the opportunity to focus on SharePoint training over the last twelve years, and for putting up with my idiosyncrasies.
➢ Microsoft - for creating such an amazing product as SharePoint!
➢ All of those who have attended my classes and have asked some of the most interesting questions - many of which led to the choice of topics and details in this book.
➢ Everyone in the MSDN, TechNet and sharepoint.stackexchange.com forums - who both ask the questions to test my knowledge of SharePoint and answer many of my dumb questions.

Preface

None needed! Turn to chapter 1 and get started!

Table of Contents

1. **Read Me First**

Welcome!

This book is for the SharePoint "power user" who needs a better understanding of how SharePoint formulas work, where they don't work, and how they are created. While at first glance SharePoint formulas appear to be simple calculations, they are both quite powerful and have weird limitations. In this book we will explore the basics of creating Calculated Columns and Validation formulas with some boring details, and over one hundred examples. We will also explore workarounds for many of the limitations by using SharePoint Designer workflows and a few tricks!

Where are formulas used in SharePoint?

- **Calculated column** formulas derive data from other columns in the same list item. These can be simple calculations and text manipulations or complex Excel-style formulas.

- **Column validation** formulas are used to create custom validations for user entered data. These can be used to make sure that quantities are not negative and vacation requests are for dates in the future.

- **Column default formulas**, while very limited, can auto-fill columns with a date 30 days in the future or a message based on the month or day of the week the item was added.

- **List / Library validation** formulas are used to check the values from multiple columns to verify the relationship between two or more columns. Examples include making sure a task start date is before the task end date, or to make sure an entry has a "price per pound" or a "price each", but not both.

Who is this book for?

Anyone who works with creating and customizing lists and libraries. These include:

- SharePoint on premise Farm Administrators
- Office 365 SharePoint administrators
- Site Collection Administrators
- Site Owners
- Power users
- Developers

What's in this book?

Well, basically everything you need to know about SharePoint list and library calculations!

- Tips and tricks that make writing formulas easy.
- What you can do with formulas, and often more importantly, what you can't do with formulas.
- Lots of the documentation on SharePoint formulas, functions and limitations.
- Over 100 examples:
    - 60+ examples of Calculated Columns.
    - 30+ examples of Validation formulas.
    - 20 examples of workarounds using SharePoint Designer workflows.

What's not in this book

Things that only programmers, or administrators with big budgets can do. We do not cover JavaScript hacks, custom code or custom web parts.

SharePoint Versions

While this book specifically targets SharePoint 2013, 2016, 2019 and SharePoint Online, very little has changed in the core formula related features as SharePoint has evolved from 2007, to 2010 and on to SharePoint Online. Most of what you learn here applies to all versions of SharePoint from 2007 to current.

About the Screen Captures and Steps

Most of the screen captures and steps are from SharePoint 2016 and Excel 2016. Unless otherwise noted, all of the examples will work all versions of SharePoint 2007, 2010, 2013, 2016, 2019 and SharePoint Online.

Many of the screen captures use the Quick Edit (Datasheet in SharePoint 2010) display of lists for the convenience of row and column outlines. This is not a requirement for any of the examples.

Extra spaces and line breaks have often been added to the formulas to add clarity. SharePoint does not require these spaces, and will remove them when the formula is saved.

Terminology

In the book we have tried to be consistent in the naming of things and roles. This can be a bit of a challenge as Microsoft's documentation and the text used in SharePoint sites are not always consistent.

Webs and Sites

Microsoft often uses the word "Site" to both describe a single site and an entire site collection. We will use the terms Web and Site, and most often Site, to refer to the SPWeb object and the term Site Collection to refer to the SPSite object. The SPWeb object represents a single site and is a container of pages, lists and libraries. The SPSite object is a container of SPWeb sites.

Users and Roles

Many organizations have their own names for SharePoint roles. We will use the Microsoft naming convention of Site Collection Administrators and Site Owners for those with "super powers" and Members and Visitors for mere users. ☺

Site Owners manage a single site, including the lists, libraries, pages, content and user permissions. The Site Owner typically has the "Full Control" permission level.

Site Collection Administrators manage features that impact the entire site collection and have access to all sites and content in the site collection. Site Collection Administrators are not by default members of any

SharePoint group or permission level. They are assigned the role of Site Collection Administrator by SharePoint server administrators, Office 365 tenant administrators or other existing Site Collection Administrators.

Members typically are assigned the Edit or Contribute permission level and can add, edit and delete content found in lists and libraries. Users with the Edit permission level can also add, customize and delete lists and libraries.

Visitors typically are assigned the Read permission level and can view and download content.

2.   **Tips for Formulas**

If you are in a hurry, go to the table of contents or the index and look for what you need. If you do have a few minutes to spare, then this is the best place to start!

Four Places to Write Formulas

You can write custom formulas for:

- Calculated Columns – Columns that display a calculated value and supports no user data entry.
- Calculated Defaults – Formulas used to create a column's default value.
- Column Validation – Formulas that return either True or False that are used to make sure the data entered in a single column matches a rule or pattern.
- Validation Settings – Formulas that return either True of False that are used to make sure the data entered in any, or all, of the columns of an item matches a rule or pattern.

Calculated Columns are not Derived Columns (An issue with TODAY())

One very important thing to remember about Calculated Columns, they are only updated when the list item is initially created, or when the list item is updated. This is why the built-in variable [TODAY] is not allowed in Calculated Columns. Some people have found a workaround by using the Excel-style TODAY() and NOW() functions, but many don't realize that the Calculated Columns are not recalculated on each view of a list.

For example, the "Calc'd Time" column below contains this simple formula:

In the results below, note that the Modified and Calc'd Time columns report the same time. The formula is not being updated each time the list is being viewed. It is only updated when the individual list items are being added or edited.

Modified	Calc'd Time
4/22/2018 9:45 PM	4/22/2018 9:45 PM
4/22/2018 9:48 PM	4/22/2018 9:48 PM
4/22/2018 9:49 PM	4/22/2018 9:49 PM
4/22/2018 9:51 PM	4/22/2018 9:51 PM

Bottom line:

The value in a Calculated Column is only calculated when the item is modified, and the result of the calculation is stored as part of the Calculated Column. This unchanging result is then displayed each time a user displays the list of items.

Excel-like Equations

SharePoint uses functions and formula syntax from Microsoft Excel. If you are a master of Excel formulas, then you have a great head start on writing SharePoint formulas. While similar to Excel formulas, SharePoint formulas are a subset of those available in Excel and have a few additional rules and restrictions.

Excel 2016 has over 470 functions built-in. Only a small subset of these can be used in SharePoint.

What does **not** work:

- Functions that only accept ranges. Two examples:
  - SUMIF does not work in SharePoint as it works only with a range of cells. (A1:A5)
    SUM works because it accepts both ranges and comma delimited lists of values.
    SUM(A1, A2, A3, A4, A5)
  - VLOOKUP requires ranges to work.
- Add-in function libraries are not supported by SharePoint formulas.

Excel Functions vs. other calculation tools you may have used:

- Excel functions do not support Boolean operators. Boolean functions are used instead:
  - AND(…, …, …)   OR(…, …, …)
- There are no variables. I.e. no way to do something like this:
  x = StartDate + 2; if(WEEKDAY(StartDate) = 7) then x = x + 3
- There are no looping statements: I.e. no for (i = 1 to 10) doSomeCode
- Text comparisons are not case sensitive.
  =OR(status = "a", status="c")   is true for either "A" or "a" or "C" or "c".
  Use the EXACT() function for case sensitive comparisons.

Tip: As you create these formulas, remember that Calculated Column formulas return a value, while Validation formulas return either a True or a False.

Column Types that cannot be used in Calculated Columns

Not all SharePoint columns are created equal… some cannot be used as a source of data for a Calculated Column or validation formula.

Unsupported column types for SharePoint formulas:

- Lookup columns.
- Multivalued columns. For example: Choice columns with the "checkboxes" option enabled.
- Multiple lines of text columns.
- Person or Group columns. (These have complex data types that store multiple values: display name and user ID.)
- Hyperlink columns. (These columns store two values: display text, and the URL.)
- Managed Metadata columns. (The data stored is not the data displayed.)
- Hidden columns. Internal columns used by SharePoint.
- Location columns. (Longitude and Latitude – can only be added using code.)
  https://docs.microsoft.com/en-us/sharepoint/dev/general-development/how-to-add-a-geolocation-column-to-a-list-programmatically-in-sharepoint

There are workarounds for some of these. See the "Workflow Workarounds" chapter.

Commas and Other Delimiters

Function delimiters can vary based on the locale settings in SharePoint. Where a locale (country) uses "," for the decimal mark, you will need to use ";" as the delimiter instead of ",".

In locales where "." is the decimal mark:

Numbers use ".":   6.00
Formulas use ",":   IF(Price > 100, "Expensive", "Cheap")

In locales where "," is the decimal mark:

Numbers use ",":   6,00
Formulas use ";":   IF(Price > 100; "Expensive"; "Cheap")

See: https://msdn.microsoft.com/en-us/library/bb862071(v=office.14).aspx#alert_caution

Writing Formulas

SharePoint does not provide fancy code editors to help you write formulas. There are no "Intellisense", auto-complete or color coding features to help you know when you have made a mistake.

When writing a Column Validation formula, you only get a simple text box, and if you make a mistake, only a vague error message.

⊟ Column Validation

Specify the formula that you want to use to validate the data in this column when new items are saved to this list. The formula must evaluate to TRUE for validation to pass.

Example: If your column is called "Company Name" a valid formula would be [Company Name]="My Company".

Learn more about proper syntax for formulas.

Formula:

When writing a Calculated Column formula or a list/library Validation formula, you get the bonus of a list of acceptable column names to choose from.

Formula

Specify the formula you want to use to validate data when new items are saved to this list. To pass validation, the formula must evaluate to TRUE. For more information, see Formulas in Help.

Example: =[Discount]<[Cost] will only pass validation if column Discount is less than column Cost.

Learn more about proper syntax for formulas.

Formula:

Insert Column:

Copy Source
Created
Date Picture Taken
IsSquare
Modified
NewID
Picture Height
Picture Width
PictureFormat
Title

Add to formula

If there are any errors, all you get is this helpful message: ☺

Sorry, something went wrong

The formula contains a syntax error or is not supported.

TECHNICAL DETAILS

GO BACK TO SITE

The Easiest Way to Write SharePoint Formulas!

SharePoint only offers a simple text editor for writing formulas. Errors are hard to spot and debug. One too few, or one too many, parentheses or commas, and all you get to help with debugging is a "Sorry, something went wrong" message. See chapter 12 to learn more about these error messages.

Excel to the rescue!

As SharePoint formulas are Excel based, one of the easiest ways to write these formulas is to use Excel. Fire up Excel, name one cell for each column used in your SharePoint formula, enter some sample data and then use Excel's formula editor to write your formulas!

As an example, we've got a list of computer stuff for sale…

Title		Category	Qty	Price
Desktop Computer ✵	⋯	Hardware	9	$1,000.00
Laptop Computer ✵	⋯	Hardware	10	$1,000.00
WordStar 1.0 ✵	⋯	Software	20	$1,000.00
500 lb box of "parts" ✵	⋯	Other	10	$1,000.00

We offer a discount if you buy in quantity… the discount varies based on the type of item.

- Buy less than 10 items, no discount.
- Buy 10 or more Hardware items and get a 30% discount.
- Buy 10 or more Software items and get a 50% discount.
- Buy 10 or more "Other" items and get a 20% discount.

The result should look like this:

Title		Category	Qty	Price	Buy'm all!
Desktop Computer ✵	⋯	Hardware	9	$1,000.00	$9,000.00
Laptop Computer ✵	⋯	Hardware	10	$1,000.00	$7,000.00
WordStar 1.0 ✵	⋯	Software	20	$1,000.00	$10,000.00
500 lb box of "parts" ✵	⋯	Other	10	$1,000.00	$8,000.00

This will need a non-trivial IF function to return the correct price. Here are the steps:

1. Open Microsoft Excel.

2. In column A enter the names of the columns needed in the formula. Do not type the square brackets used with SharePoint column names.

3. Highlight the names you entered, and the empty cells in the next column. (A2 to B4 in this example.)

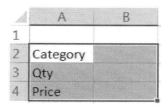

4. From the Formulas Ribbon tab, click "Create from Selection", select only "Left column" and click OK.

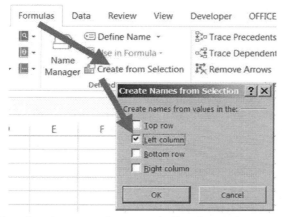

Note that there are other ways in Excel to assign names to the cells.

5. If you want to confirm that you named your cells correctly, click one of the cells in the second column and check for the cell name in the formula bar.

Note: Column names with spaces will have the spaces converted into underlines in Excel. Remember to remove the underlines and add square brackets around the column name before pasting back into SharePoint.

Column name: Price Each
In Excel: Price_Each
In SharePoint formula: [Price Each]

6. Enter some test data:

	A	B
1		
2	Category	Hardware
3	Qty	100
4	Price	650

7. Now pick an empty cell and write an equation using normal Excel rules, but use cell names instead of cell addresses:

= Qty * Price

Note: IntelliSense even helps by listing your cell names! The items in the dropdown with the "name tag" icons are the cell names.

8. Now add our first discount test – Less than 10 gets no discount, more than 10 gets the minimum of 20%. Rewrite the formula to include an IF statement.

2	Category	Hardware
3	Qty	100
4	Price	650
5		=IF(Qty < 10, Qty * Price,
6		IF(logical_test, [value_if_true], **[value_if_false]**)

IntelliSense helps again… now finish the formula:

2	Category	Hardware
3	Qty	100
4	Price	650
5		=IF(Qty < 10, Qty * Price, Qty * Price * 80%)

Note: There are several ways to write this formula! Both of the following produce the same result.

=Qty*Price * IF(Qty < 10, 100%, 80%)   or   =IF(Qty < 10, 100%, 80%) * Qty * Price

9. Do some testing to make sure the discount kicks in at Qty=10.

2	Category	Hardware
3	Qty	9
4	Price	100
5		900

2	Category	Hardware
3	Qty	10
4	Price	100
5		800

10. Let's change the formula a bit to save some repetition:

=IF(Qty < 10, 100%, 80%) * Qty * Price

11. Now write the rest of the formula to incorporate all of the rules needed by our example.

Hardware
100
650

=IF(Qty < 10, 100%, IF(Category="Hardware", 70%, IF(Category="Software", 50%, 80%))) * Qty * Price

The formula might be a bit more obvious if it is written across multiple lines. (You can do this in Excel if you expand the height of the edit box and press Alt-Enter for each new line.)

```
=IF( Qty < 10, 100%,
      IF( Category="Hardware", 70%,
            IF( Category="Software", 50%,
                  80%
      )))
   * Qty * Price
```

This is a standard Excel function… nothing special needed to use it in SharePoint!

12. Do some testing:

2	Category	Hardware
3	Qty	10
4	Price	100
5		700

2	Category	Software
3	Qty	10
4	Price	100
5		500

2	Category	Other
3	Qty	10
4	Price	100
5		800

13. Now copy the formula from Excel and paste it into a new Calculated Column in SharePoint:

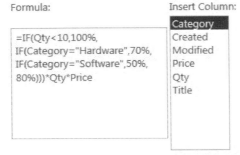

Formula:

```
=IF(Qty<10,100%,
IF(Category="Hardware",70%,
IF(Category="Software",50%,
80%)))*Qty*Price
```

Insert Column:

Category
Created
Modified
Price
Qty
Title

Add to formula

(This formula will display on one line by default. The multiple lines are used in the book so we can display the entire formula.)

Reminder: Column names with spaces will have the spaces converted into underlines in Excel. Remember to remove the underlines and add square brackets around the column name before pasting into SharePoint.

Column name:	Price Each
In Excel:	Price_Each
In SharePoint formula:	[Price Each]

14. The result:

Title		Category	Qty	Price	Buy'm all!
Desktop Computer ✕	•••	Hardware	9	$1,000.00	$9,000.00
Laptop Computer ✕	•••	Hardware	10	$1,000.00	$7,000.00
WordStar 1.0 ✕	•••	Software	20	$1,000.00	$10,000.00
500 lb box of "parts" ✕	•••	Other	10	$1,000.00	$8,000.00

Writing equations of this sort is often is a two-part process: break the problem down into pieces and then assemble and test each piece one at a time. The challenge is ending up with a single formula written as a single line of text. You can write the formula in multiple neatly formatted lines... but after saving it, SharePoint will turn it into one long single line of text wrapped inside of the formula box.

```
=IF(Qty< 10,100%,
IF(Category="Hardware", 70%,
IF(Category="Software",
50%,80%)))*Qty*Price
```

The IF and CHOOSE functions

While simple Calculated Columns can do math, such as [Qty]*[Price], more advanced formulas can be built using additional Excel style formulas.

There are several functions that can make decisions by testing values:

- IF
- IFERROR
- ISBLANK
- ISNUMBER
- ISTEXT
- ISNONTEXT
- CHOOSE

Sadly, several of the more interesting logical functions will not work in SharePoint as they require a range:

- SUMIF
- VLOOKUP

The IF function can make decisions.

=IF([State] = "OH", "Call 513-000-000", "Call 1-800-000-0000")

You can compare numbers, text, dates and true/false values, as long as the data is from a column that is accessible from a Calculated Column.

The IF function does have a few limits. These limits apply to most functions in SharePoint.

- SharePoint limits the nesting of IFs inside of IFs. SharePoint 2007 and 2010 only allow 7 levels of nesting, and 2013 and later only allows 19 levels of nesting.
- SharePoint limits the maximum length of a formula. SharePoint 2007 and 2010 only allow 1024 characters, while 2013 and later allow around one billion!
- Validation formulas have a maximum length of 1024 characters in all versions.

The trick for the nesting of many IFs is to only nest 19 at a time and return a text value, or an empty string (""), and then concatenate another 19 nested IFs that return a state name, or an empty string... repeat until done! For numbers, nest 19 IFs and then return a value or a zero, and then add (+) another 19 nested IFs. If you are using 2007 or 2010, then nest 7 at a time, and then concatenate or add another 7.

There's an example in the "Calculated Column Examples" chapter that shows how to nest IFs for fifty states.

IF(State="AL","Alabama",
if(State="AK","Alaska",
... *15 more here*...

15

if(State="LA","Louisiana",
   if(State="ME","Maine","")))))))))))))))))) &
   if(State="MD","Maryland",
and another 18 more! And then another block of 19, until your formula is completed.

The CHOOSE function can select from a list of choices.

The CHOOSE function uses an integer index value to choose one of several options. As CHOOSE starts with item 1 and not item 0, you may occasionally need to add one to the index value.

If [Status] = 1 then   =CHOOSE([Status], "red", "green", "blue") will return "red".

If [Status] = 2 then   =CHOOSE([Status], "red", "green", "blue") will return "green".

Using values of less than one and more than the number of items will return an error.

Comparison Operators

Statements like IF require an expression that returns True or False. For simple comparisons, you can use the Excel comparison operators.

The common Excel comparison operators:

Equal to	=	[State] = "NY" [Amount] = 100	
Greater than, Less than	<, >	[Amount] > 1000	100 is false, 1000 is false, 1001 is true
Greater than or equal to, Less than or equal to	<=, >=	[Amount] >= 1000	100 is false, 1000 is true, 1001 is true
Not equal to Also consider using the NOT() function	<>	[State] <> "OH" [Qty] <> 5 NOT([State] = "OH") NOT([Qty] = 5)	

While there is not an "IN" set operator, there is a workaround using "OR". See "An OR Replacement Using an Array Constant" later in this section.

Text Comparisons

The comparison operators above can be used with text comparisons with only a consideration or two:

- Text comparisons are not case sensitive.
  - [Status] = "Active" is true when Status equals "active", "ACTIVE" or "Active".
  - Use the EXACT() function for case sensitive comparisons.
- Mixed data types may result in errors or meaningless results.
  - "5" > 6 is true! So is "1" > 6
    The correct result can be returned from VALUE("5") > 6. The VALUE function converts text to numbers.
  - "4/1/2015">DATE(2015,4,3) is true!
    The correct result can be returned from DATEVALUE("4/1/2015") > DATE(2015,4,3). The DATEVALUE function converts text to dates.

Date Comparisons

The comparison operators listed above work with dates, as long as both values being compared are dates.

These are not dates!

- "01/12/2015" – this is text (but can be converted to a date)
- Monday
- June
- 2015 – this is a number (but can be converted to a date)

SharePoint functions will attempt to convert text to dates. In the table below, the first column is a Single Line of Text column with a few examples of things that might look like dates. The second column contains the function =YEAR([DateTestColumn]). Note when the formula was successful in guessing that the text was a convertible to a date. The last two are interesting… a blank is treated as 12/31/1899 and 100000 is 100,000 days since 12/31/1899. (Dates are internally stored as numbers where 1 equals one day.) Needless to say, columns that store dates should be Date and Time columns, not text!

Text	result	Text	result	Text	result
May	#Name?	4/12/2018	2,018	abc	#Name?
May 2	2,018	4/12	2,018		1,899
May 2, 2017	2,017			100000	2,173

Examples of date comparisons:

[Start Date] < [Due Date]	Earlier dates are represented by smaller numbers,

	therefore are less than later dates.
[Start Date] > DATEVALUE("01/12/2015")	Note that the text "01/12/2015" has been converted to a date using the DATEVALUE function.
YEAR([End Date]) = YEAR([Start Date])	True if the Start Date and End Date are both in the same year.
[End Date] < DATE(YEAR([Start Date]), MONTH([Start Date]) + 1, 1)	True if the End Date is before the 1st of the next month after the Start Date. If the Start Date is 4/15/2018 then the End Date must be before 5/1/2018. Note that the date is built from three parts, Year ([Start Date]), Month (MONTH([Start Date]) + 1) and Day (1).

The "Calculated Columns Examples" and "Column Validation Examples" chapters have a large number of date formula examples.

Boolean Operations - AND, OR and NOT Functions

Most computer languages support Boolean operators like AND, OR and NOT. Here's an example from C#:

if (price > 100 and qty > 10) { *do something* }

Excel and SharePoint formulas do not support these operators. They use AND, OR and NOT functions instead. The above formula in SharePoint might look like this:

=IF(**AND([Price] >100, [Qty] > 10)**, "get's discount", "no discount")

The AND and OR functions return True or False and can have multiple conditions, each that must return True or False. Here are a few examples…

Example ORs

In order to get a sales commission, the number of items sold must be 100 or more, or the price most be over $50: (actually both could be true)

=IF(**OR([Qty]>=100, [Price]>=50)**, "You get a commission!", "No commission for you.")

Or for a value instead of a message:

=IF(**OR([Qty]>=100, [Price]>=50)**, [Qty]*[Price]*0.10, 0)

Free shipping to Ohio or Indiana, else $5.00 shipping:

=IF(**OR([State] = "OH", [State] = "IN")**, 0, 5)

Example ANDs

You get overtime if you are in Category "Hourly" and the number of hours is greater than 40:

=IF(**AND([Category] = "Hourly", [Hours]>40)**, 40 * [Rate] + ([Hours]-40) * [Rate] * 1.5,
[Rate]*[Hours])

This could also be written as:

=[Rate]*[Hours] + IF(**AND([Category] = "Hourly", [Hours]>40)**, ([Hours]-40) * [Rate] * 0.5,
0)

The NOT Function

The NOT function simply reverses a Boolean value. I.e. it turns True to False and False to True. Although most expressions using NOT can be rewritten to not need it, NOT can make an expression clearer.

Example, you have twelve types of employees, and only one does not get overtime. You could test for the eleven that do, or test for the one that does not.

=IF(**NOT([EmpType] = "Salary")**, "You get overtime!" , "no overtime for you")

This could be rewritten as:

=IF(**[EmpType] = "Salary"**, "no overtime for you", "You get overtime!")

Or

=IF(**[EmpType] <> "Salary"**, "You get overtime!", "no overtime for you")

NOTs are most useful with YES/NO columns, or other functions that return True or False.

=IF([IsEmployee] = false, 1, 2)

This could be rewritten as:

=IF(NOT([IsEmployee]), 1, 2)

Or

=IF([IsEmployee], 2, 1)

Tip! Where possible, avoid testing against "true" or "false".

Note: SharePoint 2016 has a limit of 30 items in an AND or an OR. *(Not tested in other versions.)*

Shortcuts for Boolean Operations

Internally, SharePoint treats a Boolean "true" as a 1 and a "false" as a 0. You can take advantage of this to create formulas without using AND or OR functions.

The following are equivalent in a Validation formula:

   =AND([State] = "OH", [Status] = "Active", [Amount] > 100)

   =([State] = "OH") + ([Status] = "Active") + ([Amount] > 100) = 3   (I.e. all are true, or equal to 1)

The following are equivalent to create ORs:

   =OR([State] = "OH", [Status] = "Active", [Amount] > 100)

   = ([State] = "OH") + ([Status] = "Active") + ([Amount] > 100) > 0

For very simple validation formulas, the longer formulas below can be replaced by their shorter versions:

=IF([Amount] = 0, false, true)
=[Amount]   If Amount=0 then false, otherwise true.

=IF([State]="OH", true, false)
=[State]="OH"

=IF([Amount]=100, false, true)
=[Amount]-100   If Amount=100 then 100-100 is zero, or False, and everything else is True.

=IF([Amount]=100, true, false)
=NOT([Amount]-100)   If Amount=100 then 100-100 is zero, or False, and everything else is True.

An OR/IN Replacement Using an Array Constant

Excel will often let you use an array of values where you would normally use a range of cells. Arrays can be written as sets of comma delimited values wrapped inside of curly brackets.

   =VLOOKUP([StatusCode], {"a","Active"; "i","Inactive"; "c","Closed"}, 2, 0)

The array constant above defined is from "{" to "}" and represents a two dimensional table. The Excel range equivalent to this array looks like this:

a	Active
i	Inactive
c	Closed

While that is kind of cool, it does not always work in SharePoint Calculated Columns. One place it does work is with an OR function where it works much like the "IN" keyword in other technologies. The following two functions are equivalent:

A long OR:

```
=IF( OR( StateCode="OH", StateCode="KY", StateCode="IN", StateCode="IL", StateCode="MI" ),
    "Central Region", "Other" )
```

A shorter OR that kind of works like an "IN"statement:

```
=IF( OR( StateCode={"OH","KY","IN","IL","MI"} ),
    "Central Region", "Other" )
```

Which one would you rather type?

Both of the above can be used produce the following result using a Calculated Column named "Region":

StateCode	Region
xx	Other
OH	Central Region
IN	Central Region
CA	Other

Text Functions

Almost every text function from Excel 2010 is supported in SharePoint. Any function that requires a range (A1..B6) will not work with SharePoint. Notably missing is the SUBSTITUTE() function.

For details see "Online Function Documentation" at the end of this chapter.)

You can quickly check to see if a function works by adding a Calculated column to a list and adding the functions with constants. To show that the SUBSTITUTE function does not work in SharePoint, enter the function with dummy data: =SUBSTITUTE("abc","b","x"). Click OK and note the error message.

Supported Text Functions:

- General
  - CLEAN
  - CONCATENATE (but not CONCAT)
  - FIND (but not FINDB)

21

- o   LEN (but not LENB)
- Conversion
  - o   ASC, CHAR, CODE
  - o   DOLLAR, USDOLLAR
  - o   FIXED
  - o   LOWER, UPPER
  - o   PROPER
  - o   VALUE (but not NUMBERVALUE)
- Comparison
  - o   EXACT
- Search, Replace and Extract
  - o   FIND (but not FINDB) - finds position of text in a string
  - o   SEARCH - finds text by a pattern
  - o   LEFT, RIGHT (but not LEFTB or RIGHTB) – returns the left "x" or right "x" characters
  - o   MID - extracts a substring of text
  - o   REPLACE (but not REPLACEB) – replaces text
  - o   SEARCH (but not SEARCHB)
  - o   T - checks if a value is text
  - o   TEXT - format numbers and dates as text
  - o   TRIM - remove spaces from before and after text

Working with Dates

Also see "The IF, AND, OR and NOT Functions" section above to see how to compare dates.

Dates and times are an interesting challenge in both SharePoint and computing in general. The length of a year or a month is not consistent due to leap years and leap centuries. In the Calculated Columns Examples chapter and the two Validation Examples chapters, you will find tricks to find the last day of a month, to deal with leap years, to group by year or month, to find the week number, find the working dates between two dates, and many more.

For details see "Online Function Documentation" at the end of this chapter.

Dates are Numbers

Internally, dates are stored as numbers. In both Excel and SharePoint, the number 1 represents 1/1/1900.

Notes:

- Dates are stored as numbers: 1/1/1900 =1 and 12/31/8900 = 2,557,064
- And empty/blank column will be treated as a zero, or 12/31/1899.
- Entered date ranges are limited to 1/1/1900 to 12/31/8900.

- o The DATE function only accepts Year values greater or equal to 1900.
- o By using a formula, you can calculate dates back as far as 1/1/1753.
  - =DATE(1900,1,1) - 53690   equals 1/1/1753
  - =DATE(1900,1,1) - 45105   equals 7/4/1776!
- o Note: Excel does not accept dates before 1/1/1900, but will accept dates through 12/31/9999.
- What time is "1/1/2018"? It's midnight. The value stored is actually "1/1/2018 12:00 AM".

Times are a Fraction of a Date

Times are represented as parts of a day.

1/1/2018 12:00 AM	43,101
1/1/2018 12:00 PM	43,101.5
1/1/2018 9:00 AM	43,101.375
1/1/2018 12:01 AM	43,101.0006944444

When performing date math, you can add whole numbers to a date to create the next day, or fractions for parts of a day. In the example below, first column is a Date column, the second column is a number column and the fourth column is a calculation that adds the two.

1/1/2018 12:00 AM	1	1 day	1/2/2018 12:00 AM
1/1/2018 12:00 AM	365	365 days	1/1/2019 12:00 AM
1/1/2018 12:00 AM	0.25	6 hours	1/1/2018 6:00 AM
1/1/2018 12:00 AM	0.5	12 hours	1/1/2018 12:00 PM
1/1/2018 12:00 AM	0.041666667	1 hour	1/1/2018 1:00 AM
1/1/2018 12:00 AM	1.5	noon the next day	1/2/2018 12:00 PM
1/1/2018 12:00 AM			1/1/2018 12:00 AM

Tip! When writing a formula, don't worry about the exact number, like 0.041666667 for one hour, let SharePoint calculate it!

1 / 24 is the value for one hour (0.041666667).

1 / 24 * 8.5 is eight and a half hours. (also 8.5 / 24)

1 / 24 / 60 is one minute.

1 / 24 / 60 * 45 is forty five minutes. (also 45 / 24 / 60)

SharePoint Dates are Always Date AND Time

When you create a Date column you have the choice of Date and Date & Time.

Date and Time Format:

◉ Date Only   ○ Date & Time

Note the keyword "Format" in that option. Even if you select "Date Only", your users can still type, or copy and paste, a date and a time and it will be stored as a date and time. But… only the date will be displayed.

SharePoint's [TODAY] and [NOW][NOW] Variables

As noted earlier in this chapter in the "Calculated Columns are not Derived Columns" section, SharePoint's [Today] and [Now] variables cannot be used in Calculated columns. They can be used in View filters and column Validation formulas.

You can use the TODAY() and NOW() functions in Calculated Column formulas, but they are only recalculated when the list item is edited. They are not recalculated on each display of the list.

Dealing with Blank Dates

SharePoint internally stores dates as numbers, with 1 equal to 1/1/1900. That date was a Sunday. When performing math operations, SharePoint treats empty cells as 0. An empty date then becomes 12/31/1899 (or in Excel 1/0/1900, whatever that means).

When a column named "MyDate" is empty, the following formulas return these results:

=[MyDate]	12/31/1899
=TEXT([MyDate], "dddd")	Saturday
=YEAR([MyDate])	1899 (Excel returns 1900)

Any date formula that references a Saturday will also need to check to see if the column is empty.

For example, a validation formula to verify that a date is a Monday:

=WEEKDAY([SomeDate], 2) = 1

A validation formula to verify that a date is a Saturday needs a test to see if the column is blank:

=AND(NOT(ISBLANK([SomeDate])), WEEKDAY([SomeDate], 2) = 6)

Useful Date Functions

While SharePoint formulas do not support all Excel date functions, there is a good starting set built in, and we create some of our own workarounds.

DATE(*year, month, day*)	Returns the date for the specified year, month and day numbers.
	Tip! DATE() will accept out of range values and will adjust into the future with positive number or the past with negative numbers.
	If [SomeDate] is 4/15/2018 then DATE(YEAR([SomeDate]), MONTH([SomeDate]), DAY([SomeDate] +30)) returns 5/15/2018. (i.e. the Day was set to 45!)
TIME(*hour, minute, second*)	Returns the time for the specified hour, minute and second numbers. TIME supports the same "out of range" trick as DATE().
WEEKDAY(*date, return_type*)	Returns a number for the day of the week. If "return_type" is 2, then Monday is a 1 and Sunday is a 7. If "return_type" is 1, then Sunday is a 1 and Saturday is a 7. There are 10 "return_type" options.
TODAY()	Returns the current date. (For Calculated Columns this is the instant the list item was created or last updated.)
NOW()	Returns the current date and time. (For Calculated Columns this is the instant the list item was created or last updated.)
YEAR(*date*)	Returns the year part of the date as a number.
MONTH(*date*)	Returns the month part of the date as a number. (1-12)
DAY(*date*)	Returns the day part of the date as a number. (1-31)
HOUR(*date*)	Returns the hour part of the date as a number. (0-23)
MINUTE(*date*)	Returns the minute part of the date as a number. (0-59)
SECOND(*date*)	Returns the second part of the date as a number. (0-59)
DATEDIF(*startdate, enddate, unit*)	Number of complete years, months or days between two dates. "unit" equals "Y", "M", and "D". See the online Excel documentation for the "MD", "YM" and "YD" units.
	Microsoft's documentation says: "Warning: Excel provides the DATEDIF function in order to support older workbooks from Lotus 1-2-3. The DATEDIF function may calculate incorrect results under certain scenarios." (See the Excel DATEDIF online documentation.)
DATEVALUE(*text*)	Returns the Date serial number for the date text. Will display a date in a

	date formatted column and a number in a number formatted column. Examples: =DATEVALUE("1/12/2018") =DATEVALUE("January 12, 2018") =DATEVALUE("12-JANUARY-2018")
DAYS360(*startdate, enddate, method*)	Returns the number of days between two days based on a 360 day year (12 30-day months). (used for some accounting calculations) The optional "method" is set to FALSE (default) for USA and TRUE for Europe.
ROUND, FLOOR, CEILING and INT	These are actually math functions, but are useful when converting Dates and Time values to Date values. ("1/15/2018 9:00 AM" to "1/15/2018"). See "Converting a Date and Time to a Date" later in this chapter.

Missing Date Functions

Many useful functions found in Excel are not available in SharePoint. There are workarounds for some of these functions.

Missing:

Function	Use	Workaround
WORKDAYS	Calculates an end date give a start date and number of working days before or after a date, excluding weekends and holidays.	To exclude weekends see "Skipping Weekend Days" in the "Calculated Column Examples" chapter.
NETWORKDAYS	Returns the number of whole working days between start_date and end_date. Working days exclude weekends and any dates identified as holidays.	
WEEKNUM	Converts a date to a number for the week of the year.	See "Week Numbers" in the "Calculated Column Examples" chapter.

Converting a Date and Time to a Date

As you saw above, SharePoint dates are always dates and times. Even if you set a column to be "Date", users can still type, or copy and paste, Date and Time values. Columns formatted as "Date" may display as just a date, but they will still be filtered and calculated as a Date and Time.

If you are calculating the number of days between two dates you might write "[Date2]-[Date1]", which will produce the expected result if both dates are true Date values. If Date2 is "1/16/2018 6:00 AM" and formatted as "1/16/2018", and Date1 is "1/14/2018" subtracting the two will return 2.25 days, not the hoped for 2 days.

There are several ways of converting a Date and Time to a Date:

- Use the DATE function:
  DATE(YEAR([*SomeDate*]), MONTH(([*SomeDate*]), DAY([*SomeDate*]))
- Use the ROUND function:
  ROUND([*SomeDate*], 0)   (This will round up or down depending on the value)
- Use the FLOOR (round down) function:
  FLOOR([*SomeDate*], 1)
- Use the CEILING (round up) function:
  CEILING([*SomeDate*], 1)
- Use the INT function (which also rounds down):
  INT([*SomeDate*])

I prefer the INT as it is the least typing and I most often need to round down to remove the fractional part of a Date and Time.

Converting Numbers and Dates to Formatted Text

The TEXT() function is used to convert date and numeric values to a wide range of text formats. The SharePoint documentation for the TEXT function only has two trivial examples. To get a better idea of what can be done with this function see the online Excel documentation. While you can't do everything in SharePoint that can be done with TEXT in Excel, you can use most of the features.

Examples of use:

- Format a date:
  Given a Date and Time column named TheDate that contains 3/1/2018 8:45AM
    o This formula: =TEXT ([TheDate], "mmmm dd, yyyy")
      Returns: March 01, 2018
    o This formula: =TEXT([TheDate], "dddd, mmmm dd, yyyy")
      Returns: Thursday, March 01, 2018

  o This formula: =TEXT(B2,"dddd, mmmm dd, yyyy hh:mm.ss AM/PM")
    Returns: Thursday, March 01, 2018 08:45.00 AM

Examples in this book:

- Scientific Notation (and a bug workaround)
- Adding Leading Zeros to a Number
- Change Date Formatting
- Adding Special Symbols (¥, £, etc.) to TEXT() Number Formats

The formatting options are generally the same as the samples in Excel's custom format dialog box. Some of the exceptions are:

- The color options ("[Red]") are not supported.
- Fractions ("# ???/???") are not supported.
- The "*" used to "repeat the following character" is not supported.
- The Longitude / Latitude format is not supported. (=TEXT(123456,"##0° 00' 00''"))
- There's a bug in the scientific notation formats. (see Scientific Notation topic in the "Calculated Column Examples" chapter.)

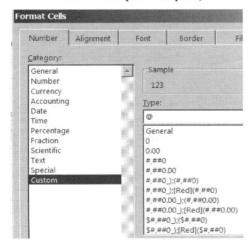

References:

- The SharePoint documentation:
  https://support.office.com/en-us/article/TEXT-function-4B46E545-E612-4C84-AC23-EDFA68007945
- The Excel documentation:
  https://support.office.com/en-us/article/TEXT-function-20D5AC4D-7B94-49FD-BB38-

93D29371225C (Click the dropdown in the "Format codes by category" section to see more options.

Math and Trigonometry Functions

Almost every math function from Excel 2010 is supported in SharePoint. Any function that requires a range (A1..B6) will not work with SharePoint. Below is a table listing some of the more common functions that are supported in SharePoint. For details see "Online Function Documentation" at the end of this chapter.

You can quickly check to see if a function works by adding a Calculated column to a list and adding the functions with constants. To show that the function that finds the number of combinations for a given number of items, COMBIN(), does not work in SharePoint, enter the function with dummy data: =COMBIN(8,2). Click OK and note the error message.

Supported Math and Trigonometry Functions:

- Rounding Functions
    - ROUND, ROUNDDOWN, ROUNDUP (but not MROUND)
    - INT, TRUNCT
    - CEILING, FLOOR
    - EVEN, ODD
- Trig Functions
    - SIN, COS
    - ASIN, ACOS
    - ASINH, ACOSH
    - ATAN, ATANH, ATAN2
- Powers and Logarithms
    - POWER
    - SQRT
    - EXP
    - LN, LOG, LOG10
- Other
    - DEGREES, RADIANS – conversion functions
    - FACT – Factorial (but not FACTDOUBLE)
    - MOD – Modulus
    - PI
    - PRODUCT
    - SIGN

Not Supported:

- RAND or RANDBETWEEN (There's a workaround in the Creating Random Numbers in the "Calculated Column Examples" chapter.

Financial Functions

Only a few of the financial functions from Excel 2010 are supported in SharePoint. Any function that requires a range (A1..B6) will not work with SharePoint. Below is a table listing some of the more common functions that are supported in SharePoint. For details see "Online Function Documentation" at the end of this chapter.

Supported functions:

- DDB
- NPER
- PMT
- PV

- FV
- NPV
- PPMT
- SYD

Statistical Functions

For details see "Online Function Documentation" at the end of this chapter.

Supported functions:

- AVERAGE, AVERSAGEA
- BINOMDIST
- CONFIDENCE
- CRITBINOM
- FDIST
- FISHER

- GEOMEAN
- HYPGEOMDIST
- MAX, MIN, MINA, MEDIAN
- NORMDIST, NORMSDIST, NORMSINV

- SUM, SUMSQ
- VAR, VARA, VARP, VARPA

- BETADIST, BETAINV
- CHIDIST
- COUNT, COUNTA
- EXPODIST
- FINV
- GAMMADIST, GAMMAINV, GAMMALN

- HARMEAN
- LOGNORMDIST
- NEGBINOMDIST
- STDEV STDEVA, STDEVP, STDEVPA

- TDIST, TINV
- WEIBULL

Online Function Documentation

For details see: https://support.office.com/en-us/article/examples-of-common-formulas-in-sharepoint-lists-d81f5f21-2b4e-45ce-b170-bf7ebf6988b3 or search for "Examples of common formulas in SharePoint Lists".

Also see the Excel function documentation for details. Keep in mind that the Excel versions of these functions often support more options. Search the web for "Excel functions (by category)" and expand the appropriate section. (https://support.office.com/en-us/article/excel-functions-by-category-5f91f4e9-7b42-46d2-9bd1-63f26a86c0eb)

The features supported in SharePoint functions have not changed since SharePoint 2010. Any online reference content, book and blog article example for SharePoint 2010 and later should work in all versions from 2010 and later.

A final note...

Just because it works in Excel does not necessarily mean it will also work in SharePoint. There are many Excel functions that are not available in SharePoint formulas.

In general,

- If the Excel function requires a range (A1..A10) then it will not work in SharePoint.
- If the Excel function is from an add-in, it will not work in SharePoint. I.e. SharePoint does not support Excel, or other, function add-ins.
- Many of the SharePoint function limits are different than Excel limits. For example, Excel can support dates through 12/31/9999 while SharePoint only support dates through 12/31/8900. (There goes my project planning calendar!)
- If you are not sure... try it. It will probably work.

3. **Calculated Columns**

In a nutshell...

Calculated Columns:

- Display a column that derives its value from data in other columns.
- Are based on Excel-like formulas.
- Can work with numbers, dates and text.
- Supports Boolean logic using AND, OR and other functions.
- Have a few unexpected limitations!

Calculated Column Restrictions and Limitations

As straight forward as they seem… Calculated Columns have a number of restrictions. While you don't need to study the details that follow, you should do a quick review to note some of the restrictions, and the features, that differ by SharePoint version.

Calculated Columns:

- Cannot be manually updated by end users.
- Cannot be directly updated by workflows.
  (Workflows can change other columns that impact Calculated columns.)
- Have a maximum of 256 characters of returned text.
- Have a maximum of 48 Calculated columns per list.
- Have a maximum equation length:
  - o 2007 and 2010 – 1024 characters
  - o 2013 and later – 1 billion!
- Have a maximum number of nested IFs:
  - o 2007 and 2010 – maximum of 7
  - o 2013 and later – maximum of 19 (there are workarounds!)

- Cannot reference:
  - Other rows/items/documents in the same list.
  - "System" columns like FileSize. (These are read only fields created by SharePoint.)
  - Lookup columns.
  - Multivalued columns. For example: Choice columns with the "checkboxes" option enabled.
  - Multiple lines of text columns.
  - Person or Group columns.
  - Hyperlink columns.
  - Managed Metadata columns.
  - The Attachments column.
  - Note: Some of the above column types can be copied by a workflow or an Event Receiver into a Single Line of Text column that can then be used by a Calculated Column.
- Cannot be totaled in Views.
  (The results of a Calculated Column can be copied by a workflow, or an Event Receiver, into a Number column that can then be totaled. See the Workflow Workarounds chapter for a solution.)
- Cannot reference "dynamic" values such as "[Today]". Calculated columns are only updated when an item is created or edited. (The TODAY() and NOW() functions can be used, but with limitations.)

Calculated columns can create formulas that return these column types:

- Single line of text
- Number (1, 1.0, 100)
- Currency ($, ¥, €)
- Date and Time
- Yes/No

Calculated columns cannot return:

- Multiple Lines of Text
- Person or Group
- Managed Metadata
- And others…

About Columns

List and library columns come in a few flavors:

- Those that you create.
- Those added by the template used to create the list or library.
- Those added by SharePoint. (File Size, etc.)

When you create a new library, you will find these six columns are visible in the Library Properties page:

Created	Date and Time
Modified	Date and Time
Title	Single line of text
Created By	Person or Group
Modified By	Person or Group
Checked Out To	Person or Group

These cannot be deleted, but you can generally edit the column title and one or two properties of each column.

When creating a new View, you will find that you have twenty-one columns to choose from:

Display	Column Name		Display	Column Name
☑	Type (icon linked to document)		☐	Created
☑	Name (linked to document with edit menu)		☐	Created By
			☐	Edit (link to edit item)
☑	Modified		☐	File Size
☑	Modified By		☐	Folder Child Count
☐	App Created By		☐	ID
☐	App Modified By		☐	Item Child Count
☐	Check In Comment		☐	Name (for use in forms)
☐	Checked Out To		☐	Name (linked to document)
☐	Content Type		☐	Title
☐	Copy Source		☐	Version

These columns are the columns you created, plus those created by SharePoint. If you use PowerShell, or write some custom C# code, you will find that there are actually 78 fields in a new Document Library. (The actual number of columns varies a bit by SharePoint version.)

There are duplicates! SharePoint fields/columns have two names, a display name and an internal name. The internal names are always unique, but the display names are often duplicated. When working with workflows you will see only the display name, and may need to do a little trial and error to pick the correct column to use!

Many of these 78 columns are:

- Derived from other columns.
- Are not well documented.
- May be for SharePoint's internal use and may have no value for most of your projects.

A sampling of the available internal columns of a Document Library:

```
App Created By    App Modified By   Approval Status   Approver Comm...  Check In Com...   Checked Out To
Checked Out To    Checked Out To    Client Id         Content Type      Content Type ID   Copy Source
Created           Created           Created By        Document Conc...   Document Cre...   Document Mod...
Document Pare...   Document Stre...   Edit              Edit Menu Tab...   Edit Menu Ta...   Edit Menu Ta...
Effective Per...   Encoded Absol...   File Size         File Size         File Type         Folder Child...
GUID              Has Copy Dest...   HTML File Link    HTML File Type    ID                ID of the Us...
Instance ID       Is Checked ou...   Is Current Ve...   Is Signed         Item Child C...   Item Type
Level             Merge             Modified          Modified          Modified By       Name
Name              Name              Name              Name              Order             owshiddenver...
Path              ProgId            Property Bag      Relink            Restricted        ScopeId
Select            Select            Server Relati...   Shared File I...   Sort Type         Source Name ...
Source URL        Source Versio...   Template Link     Title             Type              UI Version
Unique Id         URL Path          Version           Virus Status      Workflow Ins...   Workflow Ver...
```

Views and Calculated Columns

When creating a list or library View, you will find that Calculated Columns are not available in all of the column selection lists.

Calculated Columns:

- Can be displayed in Views.
- Can be used for View Filters.
- Can be used for View Grouping.
- Can be used for View Sorting.

Calculated Columns cannot:

- Be used in the Total section. (Count, Variance, Average, Maximum, Minimum, Sum, Std Deviation) There is a workaround – see the "Workflow Workarounds" chapter.

Note: The Modern UI views do not currently display View Totals like Average and Sum.

A Note About Columns and Workflows

When working with workflows, the columns available for update depend on if they are modifiable (not read-only). When using the "Set Field in Current Item" workflow action in a new Document library you will only be able to select the following list of columns. All of the other columns are read only or not modifiable by a workflow.

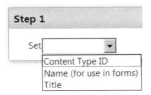

Columns that you added to your list will show up here if they are modifiable. Calculated columns will not show up here as they are not modifiable!

When reading data from columns, you will see you will find all of the list's columns. The "Field from source" dropdown includes all of the columns in the big list above.

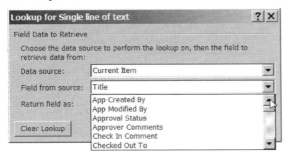

Calculated Columns can only see certain kinds of columns. (See the list in the "Calculated Column Restrictions" section earlier in this chapter.) For a new Document library, you will only see:

Most of the other columns can be used by a Calculated Column by using one of the solutions in the "Workflow Workarounds" chapter.

4. **Calculated Column Examples**

The real core of this book are the examples. In this chapter we have more than sixty examples of Calculated Columns.

Examples in this chapter:

- Fun stuff that may not work for you:
    - Add HTML to a Calculated Column
    - Add icons or pictures to a Calculated Column
    - Building an Address (String Concatenation)
    - Create a Bar Chart Column
- Columns for Views
    - View Filtering on a Calculated Column
    - Group by Year
    - Group by Month and Year
    - Group by Year Plus Month
    - Grouping on an Algorithm
- Numbers
    - Adding Leading Zeros to a Number
    - Scientific Notation
    - Roman Numerals
- The IF Function and Boolean Logic
    - Calculating a Discount using Nested IFs
    - Working Around Nested IF Limits
    - Convert from State Codes to State Names
    - ANDs and ORs - Approve if all approved, or reject if any one rejects
- Test for values
    - Testing for a Range of Dates

- o   Creating Random Messages (using CHOOSE)
- A Calculated Task Status
- Great Circle Distance from Longitude and Latitude
- Simplify a Workflow by Using a Calculated Column

Fun stuff that may not work for you!

We will start out with two examples that will not work in all versions of SharePoint, just to highlight that there are differences between SharePoint versions. Unless otherwise noted, all the other examples will work in all versions of SharePoint.

Add HTML to a Calculated Column

Developers often add JavaScript code to a page to add and manipulate HTML and icons to SharePoint pages. By using a little "trick" we can add display HTML and images to list items using a Calculated Column, and with no JavaScript needed. See "Add HTML to a Calculated Column" in the previous chapter for more details about this "trick".

> While the following trick works in SharePoint up to version 2019, it is thought of as a "bug". The "bug" has been "fixed" in SharePoint Online! It was also fixed in SharePoint 2013 and 2016 with the June 2017 update. While disabled by the update, your SharePoint server administrators can re-enable it. See: https://support.microsoft.com/en-us/help/4032106/handling-html-markup-in-sharepoint-calculated-fields

Notes:

- The two components needed to create HTML from a Calculated Column are:
  - o   A fragment of HTML to display text or an image added to the formula as a quoted string.
  - o   Setting the **Result Type** of the column to "Numeric" or "Date and Time".
- If you want to display images, you can use any web browser compatible image found in a SharePoint installation or stored in a SharePoint library. If you are a server administrator, browse the image files in C:\Program Files\Common Files\microsoft shared\Web Server Extensions\16\TEMPLATE\IMAGES (change the 16 to match your version) to see examples of what you can use in your pages.
- Set the "The data type returned" to any of the following:
  - o   Number (1, 1.0, 100)   (result will be right aligned)

      o   Currency ($, ¥, €)   (result will be right aligned)

      o   Date and Time   (result will be **left** aligned)

And now for an example…

Add icons or pictures to a Calculated Column

Note: This uses the trick / bug, "Add HTML to a Calculated Column", described above. It will not work with SharePoint Online. It will work with SharePoint 2019 and SharePoint 2013, and also with 2016 after the June 2017 patches, but only if your SharePoint administrators have allowed it! (*There is a workaround in the "Workflow Workarounds" chapter.*)

Here's a simple example that will display the same symbol (a green circle) in every row of a list:

="<img src='http://*yourPath*/_layouts/images/KPIDefault-0.GIF' border='0'/>"

It includes:

- An <img> tag.
- A URL to an image. (To a file in your library or to a SharePoint icon.) In the example above, change "yourPath" to your server URL. Something like: http://yourserver.com/sites/yourSite.
- The "_layouts/images" is the path to the built-in SharePoint icons. You can also use an image stored in a library.
- The "border" hides the default border added to an image by default. You could of also have added "style='border-style:none'".

Here's an example that uses a Single Line of Text or Choice column named "Status" that contains the text "Red", "Green" or "Yellow", combined with a Calculated column named "Status Color" that contains a mix of HTML strings and three nested IF statements.

Title		Status	Status Color
Monday ✻	•••	Green	⬤
Tuesday ✻	•••	Red	◆
Wednesday ✻	•••	Yellow	▲

Steps:

1. Add a column to your list named "**Status**". Make it a Choice list with three choices: "Green", "Yellow" and "Red".

2. Add another column named "Status Color" (any name will do). Make it a Calculated Column and set the formula to the following, but with the correct path to your site! (Change *yourPath* to something like /sites/yourSite/_layouts/images)

```
="<center>" &
    IF( [Status] = "Green", "<img src='yourPath/KPIDefault-0.GIF' border='0'/>",
        IF( [Status] = "Yellow", "<img src='yourPath/KPIDefault-1.GIF' border='0'/>",
            IF( [Status] = "Red", "<img src='yourPath/KPIDefault-2.GIF' border='0'/>",
            ""

    ) ) ) &
    "</center>"
```

3. Change the "The data type returned from this formula is" to "Number".
4. Save and test!

Here's a variation for a Task list that uses the red icon for tasks not started (% Complete = 0), the green icon for completed tasks (% Complete = 1) and the yellow icon for anything else (i.e. In Progress).

```
="<center>" &
    IF( [% Complete] = 1 , "<img src='http://yourPath/KPIDefault-0.GIF' border='0'/>",
        IF( [% Complete] = 0 , "<img src='http://yourPath/KPIDefault-2.GIF' border='0'/>",
            "<img src='http://yourPath/KPIDefault-1.GIF' border='0'/>"
    ) ) ) &
    "</center>"
```


Notes:

- Replace "*yourPath*" with your URL to the image location. For the default SharePoint icons, this might be *yourServer/sites/yourSite/_layouts/images*.
- Each IF has an ELSE that is another IF.
- The final IF has an ELSE that is an empty string (""). This blank value will be displayed if none of the colors are a match. You might replace the empty string with an error message or another icon.

Building an Address (String Concatenation)

We often enter data in discrete units like Address, City and State and then display them as a single column. Calculated Columns can concatenate (combine) text using the "&" operator or the CONCATENTATE() function. Both of the following will produce the same results:

```
=[Address] & " " & [City] & ", " & [State]
```

=CONCATENATE([Address], " ", [City], ", ", [State])

Line Breaks?

SharePoint Calculated Columns do not support adding line breaks by embedding new line codes. The result of a Calculated Column of text is a "single line of text", so that's not really expected to work. A Multiple Lines of Text column sounds like an idea, but they are not supported as a Calculated Column type. If you are not using SharePoint Online, you might be able to use the "Add HTML to a Calculated Column" trick at the beginning of this chapter. You could also use a workflow workaround that copies the Calculated Column with the HTML code into a Multiple Lines of Text Column.

Here is an example with five columns named Company, Address, City, State, Zip that includes HTML <br> line break codes:

Create a Bar Chart Column

One of the less obviously useful functions is the REPT (repeat) function. It repeats a character (or characters) "x" number of times. As REPT just generates a string of text, you would display this in a Calculated Column as "Single Line of Text".

Steps:

1. Start with a list that has a numeric column. This example uses a **Number** column named "Value".
2. Add a **Calculated** column and give it a name.
3. Set the column type to "Calculated".

4.   Enter the formula: =REPT("*whatYouWantToRepeat*", [Value])
   a.   You can use any symbol or string: "*", "$", "abc"
   b.   You may want to adjust the value to fit the space available with a little math:
        =REPT("*", [Value] / 1000)   I.e. display one star for each 1000 units.
   c.   You can use a repeated image by writing some HTML code. See the first example in this
        chapter for where this will work. (Will not work with SharePoint Online.)
        i.   =REPT("<img src='http://yourPath/yourImage.GIF' style='border-
             style:none'/>", [Value])

The "REPT" column below uses "*" while "REPT ICON" uses an image.

Value	REPT	REPT ICON
5	*****	◆◆◆◆◆
10	**********	◆◆◆◆◆◆◆◆◆◆

Columns for Views

At first glance, Views may seem to have a limited set of options for filtering and grouping data. If what you
want to do is not in one of the View designer dropdown lists, then … you need a workaround. Calculated
Columns let you create custom data that can be used to do more advanced filtering and grouping.

Examples:

   o   View Filtering on a Calculated Column
   o   Grouping on a Calculated Column
   o   Group by Year
   o   Group by Month and Year
   o   Group by Year Plus Month
   o   Grouping on an Algorithm

View Filtering on a Calculated Column

When you need to filter on the derived value of two or more columns, create a Calculated column and use
that in the list's or View's filters.

Square Pictures Only!

As an example, lets filter pictures by their shape: Square, 4:3, 16:9, etc. Picture libraries make this easy as
the they extract picture metadata as the files are uploaded.

Our first example just filters on Square or Not Square. We will follow up with an example that uses a collection of sizes. (See the "Grouping on an Algorithm" example later in this chapter to see a more complete example.) Here's a picture library before adding the filtering column.

	Name		Picture Size	File Size	Picture Height	Picture Width
	Not so square	...	508 x 221	10 KB	221	508
	Square	...	50 x 50	1 KB	50	50
	Photo of the Dog	...	1600 x 900	7 KB	900	1600

Now let's add a column just to use for a view filter.

Steps:

1. Create a Calculated Column and name it something like "IsSquare".
2. Add a calculation like this one:
   =IF([Picture Height] = [Picture Width], "Square", "Not square")

Upload a few pictures into the All Pictures view.

	Name		Picture Size	File Size	Picture Height	Picture Width	IsSquare
	Not so square	...	508 x 221	10 KB	221	508	Not square
	Square	...	50 x 50	1 KB	50	50	Square
	Photo of the Dog	...	1600 x 900	7 KB	900	1600	Not square

Now click on the IsSquare column heading and checkmark "**Square**" to filter the list.

✓		Name	Picture Size	File Size	Modified	Picture Height	Picture Width	IsSquare
		Square ⚞	... 50 x 50	1 KB	8 minutes ago	50	50	Square

Or, modify the view to and add a view filter for just "Square" pictures.

⊟ Filter

Show all of the items in this view, or display a subset of the items by using filters. To filter on a column based on the current date or the current user of the site, type **[Today]** or **[Me]** as the column value. Use indexed columns in the first clause in order to speed up your view. Filters are particularly important for lists containing 5,000 or more items because they allow you to work with large lists more efficiently. Learn about filtering items.

○ ▦ Show all items in this view

◉ ▤ Show items only when the following is true:

Show the items when column

IsSquare ▾

is equal to ▾

Square

Grouping on a Calculated Column

Views are used to create "reports" from SharePoint lists. Views can group, total, filter and format list data. One of the nice uses of Calculated columns to is to enhance the grouping features of Views. As an example, a simple view can group on a full date in a date column but cannot group on only a year or a month.

Group by Year

To group by year, just add a Calculated column that extracts the year of a Date column. The YEAR function returns a four digit number representing the year of a date value.

> =YEAR(ReleaseDate)

You will want to force the data type to Text to avoid the addition of commas to the year number. Just concatenate an empty string ("") to the result.

> ="" & YEAR(ReleaseDate)

ProdID	Product		Color	Category	Size	Retail	ReleaseDate	ReleaseYear
749	Extra 340 3D ✳	•••	Red	R/C Plane	62	$3,578.27	9/12/2015	2015
750	Extra 340 3D ✳	•••	Red	R/C Plane	44	$3,578.27	10/1/2016	2016
751	Extra 340 3D ✳	•••	Red	R/C Plane	48	$3,578.27	7/6/2015	2015
752	Extra 340 3D ✳	•••	Red	R/C Plane	52	$3,578.27	8/15/2013	2013

As a bonus, you can now filter the list by year:

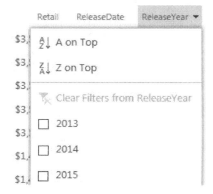

To group by year:

1. Create a new **Standard View**. (Maybe named "By Year")
2. Select the columns to display. You can uncheck the **ReleaseYear** column as it will be a bit redundant.
3. In the **Group By** section, select the new year column.

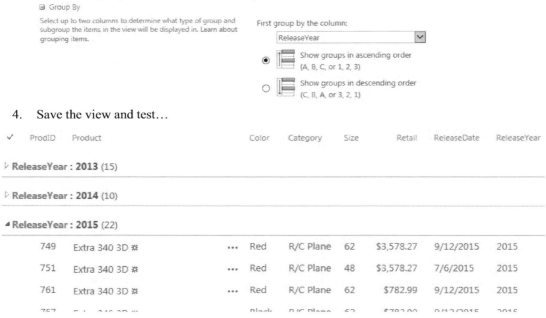

4. Save the view and test…

✓	ProdID	Product		Color	Category	Size	Retail	ReleaseDate	ReleaseYear
▷ **ReleaseYear : 2013** (15)									
▷ **ReleaseYear : 2014** (10)									
◢ **ReleaseYear : 2015** (22)									
	749	Extra 340 3D ✻	•••	Red	R/C Plane	62	$3,578.27	9/12/2015	2015
	751	Extra 340 3D ✻	•••	Red	R/C Plane	48	$3,578.27	7/6/2015	2015
	761	Extra 340 3D ✻	•••	Red	R/C Plane	62	$782.99	9/12/2015	2015
	767	Extra 340 3D ✻	•••	Black	R/C Plane	62	$782.99	9/12/2015	2015

Group by Month and Year

To also group by month just add one more column to the group by year example above.

    `=MONTH( ReleaseDate )`

To get the month to sort and group properly you will either set the **Data Type Returned** to **Number** or prefix the month text with leading zeros.

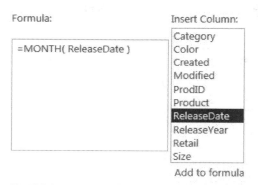

The formulas above will display the month as a number or as text:

ReleaseDate	ReleaseYear	ReleaseMonth		ReleaseDate	ReleaseYear	ReleaseMonth
9/12/2015	2015	9		9/12/2015	2015	09
10/1/2016	2016	10		10/1/2016	2016	10
7/6/2015	2015	7		7/6/2015	2015	07

The month as text used in a View group:

ReleaseYear : 2016 (14)

◢ ReleaseMonth : 04 (3)

955	3D Competition Helicopter ✻	•••	Yellow	Helicopter	50	$2,384.07	4/1/2016	2016	04
992	Silver Arrow Sailboat ✻	•••	Black	R/C Boat	48	$539.99	4/15/2016	2016	04
998	Extra 512 3D ✻	•••	Black	R/C Plane	48	$539.99	4/12/2016	2016	04

▷ ReleaseMonth : 10 (11)

The month as a number used in a View group:

⊿ **ReleaseYear : 2016** (14)

⊿ ReleaseMonth : 4 (3)

955	3D Competition Helicopter ✳	•••	Yellow	Helicopter	50	$2,384.07	4/1/2016	2016	4
992	Silver Arrow Sailboat ✳	•••	Black	R/C Boat	48	$539.99	4/15/2016	2016	4
998	Extra 512 3D ✳	•••	Black	R/C Plane	48	$539.99	4/12/2016	2016	4

▷ ReleaseMonth : 10 (11)

Group by Year Plus Month

Instead of first grouping by year, and then subgrouping by month, you may want to just group by Year plus Month.

⊿ **YearPlusMonth : 2016 - 04** (3)

955	3D Competition Helicopter ✳	•••	Yellow	Helicopter	50	4/1/2016
992	Silver Arrow Sailboat ✳	•••	Black	R/C Boat	48	4/15/2016
998	Extra 512 3D ✳	•••	Black	R/C Plane	48	4/12/2016

▷ **YearPlusMonth : 2016 - 10** (11)

▷ **YearPlusMonth : 2017 - 02** (15)

In the previous "Group by Month and Year" example you saw that we could format the month as a number or as text with a leading zero. The text version is preferred when we concatenate the year and the month for a combined grouping.

= ReleaseYear & " - " & ReleaseMonth

If we set the month to be a number, we will get an odd sort order as the text will be converted to text without leading zeros or spaces.

▷ **YearPlusMonth : 2016 - 10** (11)

▷ **YearPlusMonth : 2016 - 4** (3)

▷ **YearPlusMonth : 2017 - 11** (10)

▷ **YearPlusMonth : 2017 - 2** (15)

When using the text version of the month with leading spaces, we will get the groups in the expected sort order:

▷ **YearPlusMonth : 2016 - 04** (3)

▷ **YearPlusMonth : 2016 - 10** (11)

▷ **YearPlusMonth : 2017 - 02** (15)

▷ **YearPlusMonth : 2017 - 03** (11)

Grouping on an Algorithm

Sometimes report or view grouping needs to be done on something beyond a simple value like a Status code or a derived value like YearMonth. By using a series of IF statements, you can create all kinds of custom groupings. Building on a previous example, you may want to group pictures by their shape: square, 4:3, 5:4, 16:9, 16:10 or other ratio.

Here's a formula that will use a series of tests to assign a photo to a shape based on its height and width.

```
=IF( [Picture Height] = [Picture Width], "Square",
  IF( [Picture Height] / [Picture Width] = 0.75, "4:3",
   IF( [Picture Height] / [Picture Width] = 0.80, "5:4",
    IF( [Picture Height] / [Picture Width] = 0.5625, "16:9",
     IF( [Picture Height] / [Picture Width] = 0.625, "16:10",
  "Other" ) ) ) ) )
```

Picture libraries automatically extract image data from the image files, including the height and width needed by our formula. Here's a Picture library that that displays these extracted image data values, and our custom PictureFormat column.

	Name		Picture Size	File Size	Picture Height	Picture Width	PictureFormat
	No so square	...	508 x 221	10 KB	221	508	Other
	Photo of more Trees	...	160 x 100	1 KB	100	160	16:10
	Photo of the Boat	...	1600 x 900	7 KB	900	1600	16:9
	Photo of the Cabin	...	600 x 600	3 KB	600	600	Square
	Photo of the Cat	...	1360 x 768	5 KB	768	1360	Other
	Photo of the Dog	...	1600 x 900	7 KB	900	1600	16:9
	Photo of the Lake	...	400 x 300	2 KB	300	400	4:3
	Photo of the Mountain		1500 x 1200	8 KB	1200	1500	5:4

Even without using the View grouping feature, we immediately get a way to filter our pictures by shape.

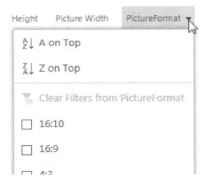

To group by shape, all that's needed is a View that groups by the **PictureFormat** Calculated column.

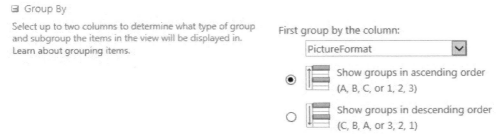

And we now have our pictures grouped by shape.

✓	🗋	Name		Picture Size	File Size	Picture Height	Picture Width	PictureFormat
▷ **PictureFormat : 16:10** (1)								
⊿ **PictureFormat : 16:9** (3)								
	🖼	Photo of the Boat	...	1600 x 900	7 KB	900	1600	16:9
	🖼	Photo of the Dog	...	1600 x 900	7 KB	900	1600	16:9
	🖼	Photo of the Trees	...	160 x 90	1 KB	90	160	16:9
▷ **PictureFormat : 4:3** (1)								
▷ **PictureFormat : 5:4** (1)								
▷ **PictureFormat : Other** (3)								
▷ **PictureFormat : Square** (2)								

Tip! If you don't like the ordering of the groups, add a prefix letter or number to the calculated values. The following will list the square pictures first, and then 4:3, 5:4, 16:9 etc…

```
=IF( [Picture Height] = [Picture Width], "A - Square",
 IF( [Picture Height] / [Picture Width] = 0.75, "B - 4:3",
  IF( [Picture Height] / [Picture Width] = 0.80, "C - 5:4",
   IF( [Picture Height] / [Picture Width] = 0.5625, "D - 16:9",
    IF( [Picture Height] / [Picture Width] = 0.625, "E - 16:10",
 "Other" ) ) ) ) )
```

Adding Leading Zeros to a Number

If you type "0002" into a Number column, it will be displayed as "2". One of the many uses of the TEXT function is to format numbers in all kinds of patterns, including with leading zeros. The following will make sure the numbers are displayed as zero padded four-digit values, except when the number has more than six digits.

```
=TEXT([SomeNumericColumn], "0000" )
```

A few samples using the above formula:

	0000
1	0001
12	0012
120	0120
2,000	2000

12,000	12000
12.5	0013
12.1	0012
-123	-0123
1,234	1234

As an alternate solution, you can use the RIGHT function and a text concatenation.

=RIGHT("000000" & [SomeNumberColumn],6)

The above is generally identical to:

=TEXT([SomeNumberColumn],"000000")

But, this is only safe to use when the number is a positive integer, and the number has six or fewer digits. Here's an example showing the differences between TEXT() and RIGHT().

SomeNumber	TEXT()	RIGHT()
123	000123	000123
123,456	123456	123456
1,234,567	1234567	234567
-123	-000123	00-123
1,234.5	001235	1234.5
0.3333	000000	0.3333

Math

When you first heard of Calculated Columns, the first thing that probably came to mind was simple math.

=[Price] * [Qty] + [Shipping]

Calculated Column math equations work identically to Excel formulas, including all of the rules for the order of evaluation. For example, if you sent someone out for lunch for your team of 10, how much money should you send along for burgers ($5) and fries ($2)?

This much?   = [burgers] + [fries] * [team members]   I.e. 5 + 2 * 10

Both Excel and SharePoint would have calculated that as $25 while you really needed to send $70! The default order of evaluation did the multiplication first, and then did the addition. I.e. 2 * 10, and then 5 + 20. To change the order of evaluation, add parentheses.

This is what was actually needed:

```
   = ( [burgers] + [fries] ) * [team members]
or = (     5    +    2   ) *  10
```

Tip! Parentheses are free! By always adding them, both the computer and the next human who reads your formula will know exactly what you wanted.

Default Order of Evaluation

—	Negation (as in −1)
%	Percent
^	Exponentiation
* and /	Multiplication and division (left to right)
+ and −	Addition and subtraction (left to right)
&	Connects two strings of text (concatenation)
= <> <= >=	Comparison

Scientific Notation

In Excel you can use the TEXT function to display very large and very small numbers in scientific notation.

$$TEXT([Number],"0.00E+00")$$

```
0.00000001  1.00E-08
3,700,000,000  3.70E+09
333,700,000,000  3.34E+11
```

There's a bug!

Due to a bug in SharePoint, the TEXT function adds some extra zeros to the end of the formatted number. (just a trivial little error!)

0.00000001	1.00E-800
3,700,000,000	3.70E+900
333,700,000,000	3.34E+1100

Here's a workaround...

Assuming you want the equivalent of Excel's TEXT([Number],"0.00E+00"):

```
=LEFT( TEXT( Number,"0.00E+00"), 6 ) &
  TEXT( MID( TEXT( Number,"0.00E+00" ), 7,
       LEN( TEXT( Number,"0.00E+00" ) ) -8 ), "00" )
```

This part:

```
LEFT( TEXT( Number, "0.00E+00" ) ,6 )
```

Pulls off the "3.70E+".

This part:

```
MID( TEXT( Number, "0.00E+00" ), 7, LEN( TEXT( Number, "0.00E+00" ) ) -8 )
```

Pulls off the "9" and formats it as "09".

Number	calc
0.00000001	1.00E-08
3,700,000,000	3.70E+09
333,700,000,000	3.34E+11

To change the format, adjust the number of zeros in the obvious places, and adjust the "6", "7" and "8" as needed. Here two examples to help you figure out which numbers to change.

For the equivalent of TEXT([Number],"0.00E+000")

```
=LEFT( TEXT( Number, "0.00E+000" ), 6 ) &
  TEXT( MID( TEXT( Number, "0.00E+000" ), 7,
       LEN( TEXT( Number, "0.00E+000" ) ) -9 ), "000" )
```

For the equivalent of TEXT([Number],"0.000E+00")

=LEFT(TEXT(Number, "0.000E+00"), 7) &
    TEXT(MID(TEXT(Number, "0.000E+00"), 8,
            LEN(TEXT(Number, "0.000E+00")) -9), "00")

Here are the "0.00E+00", "0.00E+000" and "0.000E+00" results.

0.00000001	1.00E-08	1.00E-008	1.000E-08
3,700,000,000	3.70E+09	3.70E+009	3.700E+09
333,700,000,000	3.34E+11	3.34E+011	3.337E+11

Roman Numerals

499 = CDXCIX

While this may not be your most often used Calculated Column function, it is interesting to discover some of the unexpected stuff hiding in Excel's function library!

=ROMAN([*SomeNumberColumn*])

The number must be value from 0 to 3,999.

TheNumber	Roman
1	I
3	III
9	IX
10	X
11	XI
499	CDXCIX

There's often more than one way to represent a number with Roman numerals. You can add an optional parameter to select from four other formats.

499	=ROMAN(TheNumber)	CDXCIX
499	=ROMAN(TheNumber,1)	LDVLIV
499	=ROMAN(TheNumber,2)	XDIX
499	=ROMAN(TheNumber,3)	VDIV
499	=ROMAN(TheNumber,4)	ID

If you would like to use Roman numerals in a SharePoint page, or in a Content Editor Web Part, see this article: http://techtrainingnotes.blogspot.com/2018/03/adding-roman-numerals-to-sharepoint.html

Note: Excel's ARABIC function that converts Roman numerals into numbers is not supported by SharePoint.

The IF Function and Boolean Logic

The IF function will be one of your most used SharePoint formula functions. For more on the IF function and other logic functions see the "IF and CHOOSE Functions" topic in the "Tips for Formulas" chapter.

Here are the biggest limitations of the IF function:

- Maximum nesting levels:
    o   7 for SharePoint 2007 and 2010
    o   19 for 2013 and later, including SharePoint Online
- Maximum formula length:
    o   1024 characters for SharePoint 2007 and 2010
    o   Unlimited for 2013 and later (actually, around one billion!)

Calculating a Discount using Nested IFs

As an example of nested IFs, we've got a list of computer stuff for sale…

Title		Category	Qty	Price
Desktop Computer ✳	•••	Hardware	9	$1,000.00
Laptop Computer ✳	•••	Hardware	10	$1,000.00
WordStar 1.0 ✳	•••	Software	20	$1,000.00
500 lb box of "parts" ✳	•••	Other	10	$1,000.00

We offer a discount if you buy in quantity… the discount varies based on the type of item.

- Buy less than 10 items, no discount
- Buy 10 or more Hardware items and get a 30% discount
- Buy 10 or more Software items and get a 50% discount
- Buy 10 or more "Other" items and get a 20% discount

The result should look like this:

Title		Category	Qty	Price	Buy'm all!
Desktop Computer ✻	•••	Hardware	9	$1,000.00	$9,000.00
Laptop Computer ✻	•••	Hardware	10	$1,000.00	$7,000.00
WordStar 1.0 ✻	•••	Software	20	$1,000.00	$10,000.00
500 lb box of "parts" ✻	•••	Other	10	$1,000.00	$8,000.00

As there are multiple conditions, we will need a few nested IFs to pick the discount rate.

```
=IF( Qty < 10, 100%,
     IF( Category="Hardware", 70%,
        IF( Category="Software", 50%,
            80%
     ) ) )
   * Qty * Price
```

Notes:

- The extra line breaks and spacing in this example are only for clarity. SharePoint will remove them when you save the formula.
- The outer IF checks to see if the Qty is less than 10, and if so, sets the price multiplier to 100% (you could also just type 1).
- The next IF checks to see if the Category is hardware, and if so, sets the price multiplier to 70% (or .7).
- The inner most IF checks to see if the Category is software, and if so, sets the price multiplier to 50% (or .5).
- The final else sets the multiplier to 80% (or .8).
- If this was written in a Basic like language, then the above formula might have been:

```
=IF Qty < 10 THEN 100% ELSE
    IF Category="Hardware" THEN 70% ELSE
        IF Category="Software" THEN 50% ELSE
            80%
        ENDIF
    ENDIF
ENDIF
* Qty * Price
```

Working Around Nested IF Limits

As long as your equation does not exceed the maximum formula character length (1024 for SharePoint 2007 and 2010, otherwise unlimited), you can work around the nesting limits by working with smaller batches of IFs, and then adding or concatenating the results of the batches.

Let's say you are working with SharePoint 2010 and have hit the nesting limit of seven for a formula to calculate shipping costs. The costs are defined as follows:

1. < 1 pound, free
2. 1 to 5 pounds, $3
3. 5 to 10 pounds $5
4. 10 to 50 pounds $10
5. 50 to 100 pounds $20
6. 100 to 250 pounds $50
7. 250 to 1000 pounds $100
8. 1000 to 2000 pounds $500
9. 2000 to 5000 pounds $1000
10. Over 5000 pounds $2000

One solution is to just create 10 non-nested IFs that return either a value or a zero, and just add them together. The only limitation to this approach is the maximum formula length (1024 characters in 2007 and 2010).

```
=IF( [Weight] < 1, 0, 0)        This one is redundant, but is here for clarity.
+ IF( AND( [Weight] >= 1, [Weight] < 5 ), 3, 0)
+ IF( AND( [Weight] >= 5, [Weight] < 10 ), 5, 0)
+ IF( AND( [Weight] >= 10, [Weight] < 50 ), 10, 0)
+ IF( AND( [Weight] >= 50, [Weight] < 100 ), 20, 0)
+ IF( AND( [Weight] >= 100, [Weight] < 250 ), 50, 0)
+ IF( AND( [Weight] >= 250, [Weight] < 1000 ), 100, 0)
+ IF( AND( [Weight] >= 1000, [Weight] < 2000 ), 500, 0)
+ IF( AND( [Weight] >= 2000, [Weight] < 5000 ), 1000, 0)
+ IF( [Weight] >= 5000, 2000, 0)
```

If the logic is a bit more complex, then a nested IF solution is usually a better choice. If we only had to deal with the first seven we could just write this formula:

```
=IF( [Weight] < 1, 0,
  IF( [Weight] < 5, 3,
    IF( [Weight] < 10, 5,
      IF( [Weight] < 50, 10,
        IF( [Weight] < 100, 20,
          IF( [Weight] < 250, 50,
```

```
    IF( [Weight] < 1000, 100, 500 ) ) ) ) ) )
```

Note the one closing parentheses for each IF.

Remember that SharePoint 2007 and 2010 have a nesting limit of seven. (2013 and later have a limit of 19.) To support ten levels, we can make the first seven's final ELSE value a zero and then add additional blocks of seven until we satisfy the final result. Each additional block may need an IF to exclude the values already handled by earlier blocks.

```
=IF( [Weight] < 1, 0,
  IF( [Weight] < 5, 3,
    IF( [Weight] < 10, 5,
      IF( [Weight] < 50, 10,
        IF( [Weight] < 100, 20,
          IF( [Weight] < 250, 50,
            IF( [Weight] < 1000, 100, 0 ) ) ) ) ) ) )
+ IF( [Weight] >= 1000,          Exclude values handled by the first batch.
    IF( [Weight] < 2000, 500,
      IF( [Weight] < 5000, 1000,
        IF( [Weight] >= 5000, 2000, 0 ) ) ) )
```

Only SharePoint 2007 and 2010 have the limit of seven levels. SharePoint 2013 and later support up to 19 levels.

Convert from State Codes to State Names

While the previous nested IF example returned a number, you will often use nested IFs to return text. For text you will concatenate the nested IF blocks instead of adding them. ("&" vs. "+")

If you need a formula to convert state abbreviations into state names…

- You will need 50 nested IFs,
  - but SharePoint 2007 and 2010 only allows 7, and 2013 and later only allows 19.
- You will need a little more than 1300 characters in the formula,
  - but SharePoint 2007 and 2010 only allow 1024. (2013 and later are around one billion!)

The trick for the IFs is to only nest 19 at a time and return a state name, or an empty string (""), and then concatenate another 19 nested IFs that return a state name, or an empty string… repeat until done! If you are using 2007 or 2010, then nest 7 at a time, and then concatenate another 7.

But what about 2007's and 2010's 1024 character limit? Renaming the "state" column to just one letter brings the formula down to 1111 characters, but that's still more than 1024. Solution? Leave out a few unimportant states ☺, or use three Calculated columns. The first column has the formulas for the first 25 states (in multiple IF nestings of 7 or less) and returns a state name or an empty string, The second has the next 25 states and returns a state name or an empty string. The third just concatenates the first two columns.

Here's the formula for SharePoint 2013 and later for a column named "State":
(This code is also available here: http://techtrainingnotes.blogspot.com/2018/03/a-sharepoint-calculated-column-for-all.html)

```
if(State="AL","Alabama",
if(State="AK","Alaska",
if(State="AZ","Arizona",
if(State="AR","Arkansas",
if(State="CA","California",
if(State="CO","Colorado",
if(State="CT","Connecticut",
if(State="DE","Delaware",
if(State="FL","Florida",
if(State="GA","Georgia",
if(State="HI","Hawaii",
if(State="ID","Idaho",
if(State="IL","Illinois",
if(State="IN","Indiana",
if(State="IA","Iowa",
if(State="KS","Kansas",
if(State="KY","Kentucky",
if(State="LA","Louisiana",
if(State="ME","Maine","")))))))))))))))))))) &
if(State="MD","Maryland",
if(State="MA","Massachusetts",
if(State="MI","Michigan",
if(State="MN","Minnesota",
if(State="MS","Mississippi",
if(State="MO","Missouri",
if(State="MT","Montana",
if(State="NE","Nebraska",
if(State="NV","Nevada",
if(State="NH","New Hampshire",
if(State="NJ","New Jersey",
if(State="NM","New Mexico",
if(State="NY","New York",
if(State="NC","North Carolina",
if(State="ND","North Dakota",
if(State="OH","Ohio",
if(State="OK","Oklahoma",
if(State="OR","Oregon",
```

```
if(State="PA","Pennsylvania","")))))))))))))))))))) &
if(State="RI","Rhode Island",
if(State="SC","South Carolina",
if(State="SD","South Dakota",
if(State="TN","Tennessee",
if(State="TX","Texas",
if(State="UT","Utah",
if(State="VT","Vermont",
if(State="VA","Virginia",
if(State="WA","Washington",
if(State="WV","West Virginia",
if(State="WI","Wisconsin","")))))))))))
```

ANDs and ORs

For details on AND, OR and NOT see "Boolean Operations - AND, OR and NOT Functions" in the "Tips for Formulas" chapter. Here are a few examples....

Approve if all approved, or reject if any one rejects

If you have multiple steps in an approval process, then you might have rules like this:

- If everyone one approves, then the item is approved.
- If any one person rejects, then the item is rejected.
- Otherwise, the item is in Pending status.

ver Status 6	Approver Status 7	Approver Status 8	Status
			Pending
·oved	Approved	Approved	Approved
·oved	Approved	Rejected	Rejected
·oved	Approved		Pending
	Rejected		Rejected

These rules can be best applied with an AND and an OR function.

The formula:

```
=IF(
  AND( [Approver Status 1]="Approved",
    [Approver Status 2]="Approved",
    [Approver Status 3]="Approved",
    [Approver Status 4]="Approved",
    [Approver Status 5]="Approved",
    [Approver Status 6]="Approved",
    [Approver Status 7]="Approved",
    [Approver Status 8]="Approved"), "Approved",
  IF(
  OR([Approver Status 1]="Rejected",
    [Approver Status 2]="Rejected",
    [Approver Status 3]="Rejected",
    [Approver Status 4]="Rejected",
    [Approver Status 5]="Rejected",
    [Approver Status 6]="Rejected",
    [Approver Status 7]="Rejected",
    [Approver Status 8]="Rejected"), "Rejected",
  "Pending" )
```

Testing for a Range of Dates

When writing a formula that uses AND or OR functions with the same column referenced more than once, each item the function must be a complete test that returns either true or false.

```
=IF( AND( [someDateColumn] > DATEVALUE("1/1/2018"),
          [someDateColumn] <=  DATEVALUE("12/31/2018")),
     "OK", "Must be a 2018 date" )
```

When working with dates, remember that a date column stores a date and a time, even if the column is formatted to only display the date without the time. In the DATEVALUE("12/31/2018") part of the above formula, the date used is "12/31/2018 12:00 AM". If the user typed "12/31/2018 4:00 PM" they would get the "Must be a 2018 date" message!

Here's a better way to check for the current year:

```
=IF( YEAR( [someDateColumn] ) = 2018, "OK", "Must be a 2018 date" )
```

Or if you needed a range of dates that was not a full year:

```
=IF( AND( [someDateColumn] > DATEVALUE("1/1/2018"),
     [someDateColumn] <=  DATEVALUE("3/31/2018 11:59 PM")), "OK", "Must be a 2018 date" )
```

Testing for Empty Columns

Text columns

Single Line of Text columns are easy to test to see if they are empty.

- IF(textcolumn = "", *value_if_empty*, *value_if_not_empty*)
- IF(LEN(textcolumn) = 0, *value_if_empty*, *value_if_not_empty*)
- IF (ISBLANK(textcolumn) , *value_if_empty*, *value_if_not_empty*)

As an example, consider a list with a Single Line of Text notes column with infrequently read data. As long notes wrap and tie up a lot of screen space, you may want to exclude from the View.

Product		Cost	Multiplier	Price	Note
Hammer ✖	•••	$6.50	1.500	$9.75	
Saw ✖	•••	$12.50	2.000	$25.00	Buyer must sign a release form before purchase! Just in case they do something stupid! See customer service for form LG100B.
Staples (1lb box) ✖	•••	$0.50	3.125	$1.56	Also available in five pound boxes
Screws (1lb box) ✖	•••	$0.85		$1.70	

You could add a Calculated column to check for notes, and then prompt the user to view the item if there are notes.

> =IF(ISBLANK(Note), "", "View item for notes...")

Product		Cost	Multiplier	Price	Notes?
Hammer ✖	•••	$6.50	1.500	$9.75	
Saw ✖	•••	$12.50	2.000	$25.00	View item for notes...
Staples (1lb box) ✖	•••	$0.50	3.125	$1.56	View item for notes...
Screws (1lb box) ✖	•••	$0.85		$1.70	

Notes:

- SharePoint Calculated columns cannot see Multiple Lines of Text columns. (See the "Workflow Workarounds" chapter for a workaround!)
- The "?" is a valid character in a column name.
- Instead of a long block of text like "View item for notes..." you could use a short code that your users would recognize. Maybe "Notes" or just "*".

Numeric columns

If you had a table with prices of products, and had a column with a "price multiplier", what would you want displayed if the multiplier is blank?

The cost formula is this example is: =Cost * Multiplier

Product		Cost	Multiplier	Price
Hammer ✳	•••	$6.50	1.500	$9.75
Saw ✳	•••	$12.50	2.000	$25.00
Nails (box) ✳	•••	$0.50	3.125	$1.56
Screws (box) ✳	•••	$0.85		$0.00

Is a box of screws really free? (SharePoint formulas treat and empty column as a zero.)

You could:

- Make the Multiplier column required.
- Set a default value for the Multiplier column.
- Write a Validation formula on the Multiplier column to report an error when a blank is not acceptable.
- Write a formula for the Price column to use a default multiplier value.

If the default multiplier is 2 then we could use this formula for the Price column:

```
=IF( ISNUMBER( Multiplier ),
    Cost * Multiplier,
    Cost * 2)
```

Now the screws have a Price…

Product		Cost	Multiplier	Price
Hammer ✳	•••	$6.50	1.500	$9.75
Saw ✳	•••	$12.50	2.000	$25.00
Nails (box) ✳	•••	$0.50	3.125	$1.56
Screws (box) ✳	•••	$0.85		$1.70

Date Columns

Empty dates are treated as "12/31/1899". You will always want to test for a blank value in any formula that uses a date column. See the "Working with Dates" section of the "Tips for Formulas" chapter.

As an example, [SomeDate] + 30   returns "1/30/1900" when SomeDate is blank. Then can be solved with:

    IF(ISBLANK([SomeDate]) , "", [SomeDate] + 30)

Or with a message:

    IF(ISBLANK([SomeDate]) , "missing date!", [SomeDate] + 30)

Notes:

- The MIN, MAX, MINA and MAXA functions by default ignore empty values.

Testing for Errors

A calculated column that uses values from other calculated columns often needs to deal with errors reported in the other columns. As an example, the "MyCalculatedColumn" column below is reporting an error. The next column over is also displaying an error, even though it is not the cause of the error.

Value1	Value2	SomeCalculatedColumn	Formula
1	1	1	4
1		#DIV/0!	#DIV/0!
1	0	#DIV/0!	#DIV/0!

To deal with the issue, add an error check to the final column.

Change:

    =MyCalculatedColumn + 3

To:

    =IF(ISERR([MyCalculatedColumn]), "check your numbers!", [MyCalculatedColumn] + 3)

Value1	Value2	SomeCalculatedColumn	Formula
1	1	1	4
1		#DIV/0!	check your numbers!
1	0	#DIV/0!	check your numbers!

Better solutions?

- Add a validation formula to the Value2 column to make sure the value is not blank or a zero.
- Add an ISERR() check to the MyCalculatedColumn column to report the error.

Summing and Counting Columns

The Excel COUNT, COUNTA and SUM functions were designed to work with ranges of cells, or with a comma delimited list of cells, that could include both numeric and non-numeric data. These functions may not work as first expected in SharePoint where we only work with columns with predefined data types.

Here's an example that will pretty much work as expected. We have a trade show event where employees volunteer to cover certain days, and we need to track both the number of days and the number of hours worked.

Title		Day01	Day02	Day03	Day04
Sam ✳	•••	4	8	8	
Alice ✳	•••	2			

The formula for "Total Hours" looks like it should use SUM, while "Total Days" looks like it should use a COUNT.

Formula:	Insert Column:	Formula:	Insert Column:
	Created		Created
=SUM(Day01, Day02, Day03, Day	Day01	=COUNT(Day01, Day02, Day03, I	Day01
	Day02		Day02
	Day03		Day03
	Day04		Day04

Looks good!

Title		Day01	Day02	Day03	Day04	Total Hours	Total Days
Sam ✳	•••	4	8	8		20	3
Alice ✳	•••	2				2	1

Then someone asks if we can add some text to the columns to record vacation days as "Vac" as still they get credit for "Total Days". To do this we need to change the column types for the days to Single Line of Text. We try it, but SUM and COUNT no longer work as the values are no longer numbers.

Title		Day01	Day02	Day03	Day04	Total Hours	Total Days
Sam ✳	•••	4	8	8		0	0
Alice ✳	•••	2	Vac			0	0

The Excel COUNTA function counts non-empty values, so we should be able to quickly fix the "Total Days" column.

Formula: Insert Column:

=COUNTA(Day01, Day02, Day03   Created
Day01
Day02

And that works just fine.

Title		Day01	Day02	Day03	Day04	Total Hours	Total Days
Sam ✳	•••	4	8	8		0	3
Alice ✳	•••	2	Vac			0	2

The SUM is a bit more complicated to fix. The Excel SUMIF looks like a possibility, but it does not work in SharePoint formulas as it only uses cell ranges. We will need to write a formula for each column and then wrap them up in a SUM. Each column formula will check to see if the value is a number, and if so, will use that number, otherwise we will use zero as the value. As the column values are text, we will need to convert them to numbers using either the VALUE function or just by adding them to zero.

```
=SUM(IF( ISNUMBER( 0 + Day01 ), 0 + Day01, 0),
      IF( ISNUMBER( 0 + Day02 ), 0 + Day02, 0),
      IF( ISNUMBER( 0 + Day03 ), 0 + Day03, 0),
      IF( ISNUMBER( 0 + Day04 ), 0 + Day04, 0)  … and so on… )
```

And now we have our counts. Note: The SUM function has a limit of 30 values.

Title		Day01	Day02	Day03	Day04	Total Hours	Total Days
Sam ✳	•••	2	8	8	8	26	4
Alice ✳	•••	2	Vac		8	10	3

You will often use this style of writing formulas to squeeze the Excel square peg into the SharePoint round hole!

Counting Yes/No Columns

There are two ways to create a Yes/No column, use the Yes/No column type, or use a Choice column with the two choices of "Yes" and "No". The Choice column gives you the flexibility to offer more than two choices (Yes/No/na), the ability to use other terms such as "On" and "Off", and the option to not default to either "Yes" or "No".

Counting Yes/No columns

As an example of counting "yes" values, there are five job interview questions you must answer as either Yes or No, and if you answer Yes to three or more of the questions then you are qualified for the job.

Name		Q1	Q2	Q3	Q4	Q5	Qualified?
Fred ✳	...	No	Yes	No	Yes	Yes	You are qualified!
Richard ✳	...	No	No	Yes	No	Yes	This is not for you...

As Yes/No column values are treated by SharePoint formulas as both the Boolean values "true" and "false", and as the numbers 1 and 0, we can just add them up. Assuming our columns have names like "Q1" and "Q2" then:

$$Q1 + Q2 + Q3 + Q4 + Q5$$

Yes + Yes + Yes + Yes + Yes = 5!

We can then use an IF statement to check the total.

=IF(Q1+Q2+Q3+Q4+Q5 >= 3, "You are qualified!", "This is not for you...")

Counting Choice Columns that use "Yes" and "No" Choices

As we cannot add up text values, we will need to create a logic test. There are two ways to do this:

Lots of IF's:

= IF(Q1="Yes", 1, 0) + IF(Q2="Yes", 1, 0) + IF(Q3="Yes", 1, 0) + IF(Q4="Yes", 1, 0)
  + IF(Q5="Yes", 1, 0)

Or remembering that "true" is also treated as a one:

= (Q1="Yes") + (Q2="Yes") + (Q3="Yes") + (Q4="Yes") + (Q5="Yes")

    true   +   true   +   true   +   true   +   true = 5!

So, like the prior example, you just need to select "Yes" from at least three Choice columns to get the job.

Name		Q1	Q2	Q3	Q4	Q5	Qualified?
Fred #	...	No	No	Yes	Yes	Yes	You are qualified!
Richard #	...	No	Yes	Yes	No	No	This is not for you...

To get the "Qualified?" column we need to wrap one of the above counting solutions in an outer IF function:

    =IF(IF(Q1="Yes", 1, 0) + IF(Q2="Yes", 1, 0) + IF(Q3="Yes", 1, 0) + IF(Q4="Yes", 1, 0)
    + IF(Q5="Yes", 1, 0) >= 3, "You are qualified!", "This is not for you...")

Or using the "true" equals one trick:

    =IF((Q1="Yes") + (Q2="Yes") + (Q3="Yes") + (Q4="Yes") + (Q5="Yes") >= 3,
    "You are qualified!", "This is not for you...")

Average

At first glance, you might think that SharePoint formulas would not support the Excel AVERAGE function, as it normally uses ranges. In addition to ranges, AVERAGE will also accept a comma delimited list of values.

    =AVERAGE(1, 2, 3, 4, 5)

Knowing that fact, we can then write an AVERAGE formula something like this:

    =AVERAGE([Column1], [Column2], [Column3], [Column4])

An example:

Life is never that simple. People want to not enter numbers, or want to enter "na" or "n/a". In the example that follows we have six columns that need to support values from 1 to 4 and either a blank column or a column with "na" for missing values.

Option 1 – Only accept numbers:

If the column types are Number and a blank is acceptable for "na", then this will work:

    =AVERAGE(Column1,Column2,Column3,Column4,Column5,Column6)

You should also add a validation rule to each column to only allow blank, 1, 2, 3 or 4.

The result might look like this:

Column1	Column2	Column3	Column4	Column5	Column6	Average
1	1	1	1	1	1	1
2		2		2		2
3	3					3
1	2	4	4	4	4	3.16666666666667
						#DIV/0!

Option 2 – Allow numbers or "na":

If "na" is needed, or preferred, then the column types should be set to "Single Line of Text", with a default of "na" and a validation rule that only accepts "na", "1", "2", "3" or "4". The formula will then covert the text into numbers, if possible, and then calculate the average by taking the sum of the numbers and dividing by the count of the numbers. (Those pesky "na" values sure add a lot of work!)

```
=SUM(
  IF( ISNUMBER( VALUE(Column1) ), VALUE(Column1), 0 ),
  IF( ISNUMBER( VALUE(Column2) ), VALUE(Column2), 0 ),
  IF( ISNUMBER( VALUE(Column3) ), VALUE(Column3), 0 ),
  IF( ISNUMBER( VALUE(Column4) ), VALUE(Column4), 0 ),
  IF( ISNUMBER( VALUE(Column5) ), VALUE(Column5), 0 ),
  IF( ISNUMBER( VALUE(Column6) ), VALUE(Column6), 0 ) )
/
  (
  IF( ISERROR(Column1 / 1), 0, 1 ) +
  IF( ISERROR(Column2 / 1), 0, 1 ) +
  IF( ISERROR(Column3 / 1), 0, 1 ) +
  IF( ISERROR(Column4 / 1), 0, 1 ) +
  IF( ISERROR(Column5 / 1), 0, 1 ) +
  IF( ISERROR(Column6 / 1), 0, 1 )
  )
```

The result might look like this:

Column1	Column2	Column3	Column4	Column5	Column6	Average
1	1	1	na	na	1	1
2	na	2	na	2	na	2
1	1	1	1	1	na	1
na	na	na	na	1	na	1
na	na	na	na	na	na	#DIV/0!

Here's the validation settings each column for the Single Line of Text version:

☑ Column Validation

Specify the formula that you want to use to validate the data in this column when new items are saved to this list. The formula must evaluate to TRUE for validation to pass.

Example: If your column is called "Company Name" a valid formula would be [Company Name]="My Company".

Learn more about proper syntax for formulas.

Type descriptive text that explains what is needed for this column's value to be considered valid.

Formula:

```
=OR(Column1={"na","1","2","3","4"})
```

User message:

Must be "na", "1", "2", "3" or "4"

Note: SUM has a limit of 30 values.

MIN and MAX

Like the other statistical functions available in SharePoint, MIN and MAX can only work on columns in the same list item. They cannot work across multiple rows. MIN and MAX only return the smallest or largest value found from the list of columns, but cannot tell us which column that value was found in. (But we do have a formula for that!)

About MIN and MAX:

- Only works with numbers, not text.

- Will work with text that represents numbers. I.e. =MIN("213", "123") works and returns 123.
- Empty values are ignored.
- If all values are empty, a zero is returned.
- MINA and MAXA accept numbers, text that represents numbers and Boolean (true, false) values. A True = 1 while a False =0
- Excel 2016's MINDIFS and MAXIFS are not supported in SharePoint. (They require ranges.)

As a first example of MIN and MAX, let's look at the cost of products based on bids from vendors. If we have three Number or Currency columns named Vendor A, Vendor B and Vendor C, we can pick the lowest bidder using:

=MIN([Vendor A], [Vendor B], [Vendor C])

Here's the result:

Product		Component	Vendor A	Vendor B	Vendor C	Cost
Boat ✻	•••	Hull	$1,000.00	$900.00	$1,200.00	$900.00
Boat ✻	•••	Sail	$500.00	$600.00	$650.00	$500.00
Boat ✻	•••	Keel	$300.00	$300.00	$400.00	$300.00
Boat ✻	•••	Fittings	$350.00	$275.00	$225.00	$225.00
Boat ✻	•••	Radio	$200.00		$250.00	$200.00

Note that Vendor B did not bid on the Radio and the empty value was ignored. If you typed a zero for Vendor B, then MIN would select their bid with a price of $0.00.

Reporting the Lowest Bidder

While MIN and MAX return the smallest and largest values from the list of values, they do not return which one is the lowest or largest value, which could be useful if you wanted to know which bidder was the lowest. We can discover the winning bidder by writing a formula that compares each vendor's bid to the winning bid. Note that if there is a tie, the left most vendor will win.

```
=IF( Cost=[Vendor A], "Vendor A",
  IF( Cost=[Vendor B], "Vendor B",
    "Vendor C"
  )
)
```

Now we can see who the lowest bidder is for each component.

Product		Component	Vendor A	Vendor B	Vendor C	Cost	Winner
Boat ✳	•••	Hull	$1,000.00	$900.00	$1,200.00	$900.00	Vendor B
Boat ✳	•••	Sail	$500.00	$600.00	$650.00	$500.00	Vendor A
Boat ✳	•••	Keel	$300.00	$300.00	$400.00	$300.00	Vendor A
Boat ✳	•••	Fittings	$350.00	$275.00	$225.00	$225.00	Vendor C
Boat ✳	•••	Radio	$200.00		$250.00	$200.00	Vendor A

Combining Text Columns

You can combine multiple text columns to create addresses, names and other strings.

Use the ampersand or the CONCATENATE function to combine text columns or individual strings of quoted text. You will usually need to add spaces and commas to the results. Literal text goes in quotes.

Note: The Excel 2016 TESTJOIN() function is not supported by SharePoint.

Display First Name and Last Name in a Single Column

Merging two text columns is as simple as these formulas:

- = FirstName & LastName
- = CONCATENATE(FirstName, LastName)

As computers just do what we tell them to do, we will get the names combined without spaces.

LastName		FirstName	Initial	Full Name
Smith ✳	•••	Mike		MikeSmith
Jones ✳	•••	Sam	A	SamJones

So, let's add a space between the names.

- = FirstName & " " & LastName
- = CONCATENATE(FirstName, " ", LastName)

LastName		FirstName	Initial	Full Name
Smith ✳	•••	Mike		Mike Smith
Jones ✳	•••	Sam	A	Sam Jones

Now let's add the middle initial.

- = FirstName & " " & Initial & ". " & LastName
- = CONCATENATE(FirstName, " ", Initial, ". ", LastName)

Which works great, unless there's no middle initial.

LastName		FirstName	Initial	Full Name
Smith ✳	•••	Mike		Mike . Smith
Jones ✳	•••	Sam	A	Sam A. Jones

We need to add some logic to deal with the middle initial, the extra space and the period. You can write this formula several ways, all of which produce the same result. Pick the one that makes the most sense to you.

- = FirstName & " " & IF(Initial = "", "", Initial & ". ") & LastName
- = CONCATENATE(FirstName, " ", IF(Initial = "", "", Initial & ". "), LastName)
- = IF(Initial = "", FirstName & " " & LastName, FirstName & " " & Initial & ". " & LastName)
- = IF(Initial = "", CONCATENATE(FirstName, " ", LastName), CONCATENATE(FirstName, " ", Initial, " ", LastName))

LastName		FirstName	Initial	Full Name
Smith ✳	•••	Mike		Mike Smith
Jones ✳	•••	Sam	A	Sam A. Jones

Creating Title Capitalization

There are some simple sounding requests that can create large, impossible, or at least impractical formulas. Take the example of converting text into "title case"…

Titles of articles, books, chapters, etc. typically follow a set of rules. (Although no one seems to agree on a single set of rules.) For our example we will use the following rules for our formula. I'll leave it to you to figure out which rules to follow. :-)

- The first word is always capitalized.
- Articles are in lowercase, except for first words.
  - a, an, the
- Short prepositions are in lowercase, except for first words. (The definition of "short" varies!)

  o in, with, from, for, until, on, of, at, to

As a start for the formula we can use the Excel PROPER function. While it is close, it converts the first letter of every word to upper case, including the "short" words. PROPER("The quick brown fox jumps over the lazy dog") returns "The Quick Brown Fox Jumps Over The Lazy Dog".

Now we need to fix "over" and "the" to get our correct title case. As an Excel user you might think of using the SUBSTITUTE function, but you would quickly discover that that function is not supported in SharePoint. (*Why, oh why?*) So, we have to create a painful combination of the REPLACE and FIND functions. REPLACE can replace a group of characters by specifying a starting location, number of characters and the replacement text. FIND is used to find the starting location of the text we want to replace. (*For a workflow-based solution see the "Workaround for the SUBSTITUTE Function" example in the "Workflow Workarounds" chapter.*)

If we could use SUBSTITUTE then we might start with something like this:

```
SUBSTITUTE( MID(PROPER( Title ),1,9999),"Of","of")
```

And then nest them with a final function that looks like this:

```
=UPPER(LEFT(D29,1))&
 SUBSTITUTE(
  SUBSTITUTE(
   SUBSTITUTE(
    SUBSTITUTE(
     SUBSTITUTE(
      SUBSTITUTE(
       SUBSTITUTE(
        SUBSTITUTE(
          MID(PROPER( Title, 2, 9999),
        "The","the"),
        "Over","over"),
       "A","a"),
      "An","an"),
     "In","in"),
    "To","to"),
   "On","on"),
  "At","at")
```

The SUBSTITUTE can be replaced with a REPLACE function, but that would only replace the first occurrence. The solution using REPLACE() will require at least one column for each word we want to force to lower case. Here's the list of columns needed for only 7 replacement words:

Column	Contents
BookTitle	the adventures of huckleberry finn
TCase1 "on"	=IFERROR(REPLACE(PROPER(BookTitle),FIND(" On ",PROPER(BookTitle)),4," on "),PROPER(BookTitle))
TCase2 "the"	=IFERROR(REPLACE(TCase1,FIND(" The ",TCase1),5," the "),TCase1)
TCase3 "a"	=IFERROR(REPLACE(TCase2,FIND(" A ",TCase2),3," a "),TCase2)
TCase4 "to"	=IFERROR(REPLACE(TCase3,FIND(" To ",TCase3),4," to "),TCase3)
TCase5 "of"	=IFERROR(REPLACE(TCase4,FIND(" Of ",TCase4),4," of "),TCase4)
TCase6 "and"	=IFERROR(REPLACE(TCase5,FIND(" And ",TCase5),5," and "),TCase5)
TCase7 "in"	=IFERROR(REPLACE(TCase6,FIND(" In ",TCase6),4," in "),TCase6)
BookTitleCase	=UPPER(LEFT(TCase7,1))&MID(TCase7,2,999)

Each of the replacement columns follows this pattern:

- The IFERROR function is to deal with the "#VALUE!" returned by FIND when no match is found. If there's an error, we just select the results from the previous column.
- The FIND function searches for the replacement word with spaces appended so we don't find matches in the middle of another word.
- The first parameter of the REPLACE is the text being updated.
- The second parameter of the REPLACE is the starting point of the replace (found using FIND).
- The third parameter of the REPLACE is the number of characters to replace. (I.e. 4 for " of ")
- The fourth parameter of the REPLACE is the lowercase version of the word.

Here are the SharePoint columns for a few book titles:

BookTitle		TCase1	TCase2	TCase3	TCase4	TCase5	TCase6	TCase7	BookTitleCase
the adventures of huckleberry finn ✼	•••	The Adventures Of Huckleberry Finn	the Adventures Of Huckleberry Finn	the Adventures Of Huckleberry Finn	the Adventures Of Huckleberry Finn	the Adventures of Huckleberry Finn	the Adventures of Huckleberry Finn	the Adventures of Huckleberry Finn	The Adventures of Huckleberry Finn
the adventures of tom sawyer ✼	•••	The Adventures Of Tom Sawyer	the Adventures Of Tom Sawyer	the Adventures Of Tom Sawyer	the Adventures Of Tom Sawyer	the Adventures of Tom Sawyer	the Adventures of Tom Sawyer	the Adventures of Tom Sawyer	The Adventures of Tom Sawyer
a connecticut yankee in king arthur's court ✼	•••	A Connecticut Yankee In King Arthur'S Court	A Connecticut Yankee In King Arthur'S Court	A Connecticut Yankee In King Arthur'S Court	A Connecticut Yankee In King Arthur'S Court	A Connecticut Yankee In King Arthur'S Court	A Connecticut Yankee In King Arthur'S Court	A Connecticut Yankee in King Arthur'S Court	A Connecticut Yankee in King Arthur'S Court

You will most likely only display the final column in your list view. Here are a few more examples:

BookTitle	BookTitleCase
the adventures of huckleberry finn	The Adventures of Huckleberry Finn
the adventures of tom sawyer	The Adventures of Tom Sawyer
a connecticut yankee in king arthur's court	A Connecticut Yankee in King Arthur'S Court
the prince and the pauper	The Prince and The Pauper
the innocents abroad	The Innocents Abroad
life on the mississippi	Life on the Mississippi
pudd'nhead wilson	Pudd'Nhead Wilson
the diary of adam and eve	The Diary of Adam and Eve
letters from the earth: uncensored writings	Letters From the Earth: Uncensored Writings
the complete short stories of mark twain	The Complete Short Stories of Mark Twain

Note that one of the "The" words was not replaced in "The Prince and The Pauper" as REPLACE+FIND only updates the first match. You could fix this by adding seven more columns, TCase8 to TCase14, to catch the second set of words.

Also note that PROPER() has problems with single quotes: "Author'S". You could add another replace column to fix this.

I realize this is not an ideal solution, but it shows what can be accomplished with a limited tool set and a bit of brute force.

Return the Right Data Type!

Calculated Columns can return multiple "data type returned" types.

The data type returned from this formula is:

- ⦿ Single line of text
- ○ Number (1, 1.0, 100)
- ○ Currency ($, ¥, €)
- ○ Date and Time
- ○ Yes/No

If your date calculation is supposed to return a new date, make sure you select "Date and Time". Internally, SharePoint stores dates as numbers, so if you return Single line of text, Number, Currency or Yes/No, you will get a number as a result, not a date.

The select format also sets the text alignment. Single Line of Text results are left aligned while Number, Currency and Date/Time are right aligned.

Functions that reformat dates as words, like the TEXT() function, should always be returned as Single line of text.

Date Math

Dates are internally stored as numbers, which makes calculating dates pretty straight forward. If you are curious, day 0 is 12/30/1899 and dates before 12/30/1899 are stored as negative numbers.

Dates plus a number:

DateCol1	Plus 5	Plus 0.25	Plus 5 minutes	Plus 1 hour
10/1/2017	10/6/2017 12:00 AM	10/1/2017 6:00 AM	10/1/2017 12:05 AM	10/1/2017 1:00 AM

Dates subtracted and added:

DateCol1	DateCol2	Date2 Minus Date1
10/1/2017	10/5/2017	4

Formula	Result
= DateCol1 + 5	Five days in the future.
= DateCol1 + 0.25	6 hours in the future. (1 day = 24 hours, 1 hour = 1/24 or 0.041666667, 1 minute = 1/24/60 or 0.000694444)
= DateCol1 - 2	Two days in the past.
= DateCol2 - DateCol1	Number of days between the two dates.
= DateCol1 + DateCol2	Usually a meaningless result. As dates are internally stored as numbers, the two numbers can be added. 10/1/2017 + 10/5/2017 = 7/8/2135 Internally: 10/1/2017 = 43,009 and 10/5/2017 = 43,013, so 86,022 equals 7/8/2135 :-)

Subtracting Dates

Here's an example of subtracting two dates in a Task list to calculate the duration of the task.

=[Due Date] - [Start Date] + 1

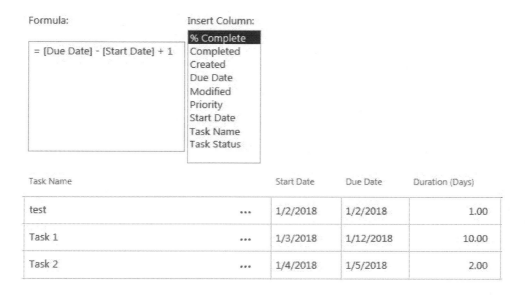

This works nicely for full day tasks, but what about partial days? What about working days? And I hope you don't ask about holidays! *(Keep reading!)*

Date Functions

DATEDIF

Most of the Excel date functions are available in SharePoint formulas. The first that we will take a look at is DATEDIF, which returns the number of years, months or days between two dates.

DATEDIF(*start_date, end_date, unit*)

The "unit" values are:

- Y for years
- M for months
- D for days

- YM, YD – These are used to calculate the number of months or days while ignoring the years. For example, using "YD" you would find that there are 4 days between "12/1/2015" and "12/5/2015", and also only 4 days (ignoring years) between "12/1/2015" and "12/5/2018".
- There is also an "MD" unit, but Microsoft says don't use it due to "known limitations".

If [Start Date] contains "3/1/2018" and [End Date] contains "5/15/2019":

=DATEDIF([Start Date], [Due Date], "y")   returns 1

=DATEDIF([Start Date], [Due Date], "m")   returns 14

=DATEDIF([Start Date], [Due Date], "d")   returns 440

=DATEDIF([Start Date], [Due Date], "yd")   returns 75

=DATEDIF([Start Date], [Due Date], "ym")   returns 2

Whole units are used. Note the difference using "3/16/2018" and "5/15/2019".

=DATEDIF([Start Date], [Due Date], "y")   returns 1

=DATEDIF([Start Date], [Due Date], "m")   returns 13

=DATEDIF([Start Date], [Due Date], "d")   returns 425

=DATEDIF([Start Date], [Due Date], "yd")   returns 60

=DATEDIF([Start Date], [Due Date], "ym")   returns 1

Dealing with Date Function Errors

If the result of the date subtraction is negative, i.e. the start_date is greater than the end_date, the result will be #NUM!.

This function returns the difference between two dates:

=DATEDIF(created, [Sold On],"d")

It returns an error if the result is negative, so use an IF and in the second DATEDIF in the IF reverse the order of the dates.

=IF(created<[Sold On],
    DATEDIF(created, [Sold On],"d"),
    DATEDIF([Sold On],created,"d")   )

YEAR(), MONTH() and DAY()

The YEAR, MONTH and DAY functions return numbers. While this is great when doing further math, years (2018) will be displayed with commas (2,018). Use the TEXT function to when you want the year without commas: =TEXT(yourDateColumn, "yyyy")

If a list item was created on 12/15/2017 then:

=YEAR([Created])   returns 2,017

=MONTH([Created])   returns 12

=DAY([Created])   returns 15

=TEXT([Created] , "yyyy")   returns 2017

Finding a Date One Year in the Future

You could just add 365 to the value in a column, or use the DATE function to build a future date.

=[yourDateColumn] + 365

or

=DATE(YEAR([yourDateColumn]) + 1, MONTH([yourDateColumn]), DAY([yourDateColumn])

What about leap years?

Leap year dates like 2/29/2016 can be a problem, so here's a little better solution. If you want 2/29/2016 to be mapped to 3/1/2017 (no adjustment for leap year) then:

=DATE(YEAR([yourDateColumn]) + 1 ,MONTH([yourDateColumn]), DAY([yourDateColumn]))

If you want 2/29/2016 to be mapped to 2/28/2017 (last date of the same month in the next year) then:

=DATE(YEAR([yourDateColumn]) + 1, MONTH([yourDateColumn]), DAY([yourDateColumn])) -

    IF(AND(MONTH([yourDateColumn]) = 2, DAY([yourDateColumn]) = 29), 1, 0)

yourDateColumn	No adjustment	Adjust for the 29th
2/28/2016	2/28/2017	2/28/2017
2/29/2016	3/1/2017	2/28/2017
3/1/2016	3/1/2017	3/1/2017

What about 1 year in the future, but on the first or last day of the month?

If you want to calculate the 1st day of the same month in the next year then:

=DATE(YEAR(yourDateColumn) + 1, MONTH(yourDateColumn), 1)

If you want to calculate the last day of the same month in the next year then: (leap year is properly dealt with)

=DATE(YEAR(yourDateColumn) + 1, MONTH(yourDateColumn) + 1, 1) - 1

yourDateColumn	First of Month	Last day of month
2/29/2016	2/1/2017	2/28/2017
2/28/2015	2/1/2016	2/29/2016
3/10/2016	3/1/2017	3/31/2017
2/28/2020	2/1/2021	2/28/2021

Change Date Formatting

SharePoint columns do not offer much in the way of date formatting.

Date and Time Format:

○ Date Only   ⦿ Date & Time

Display Format:

⦿ Standard   ○ Friendly

WARNING! If you set your date column to "Date Only" and a user enters a date and a time, the full date and time is stored and a "Date Only" version is displayed. This can impact your Calculated Columns that are assuming an exact date.

The TEXT Function

The TEXT function lets you covert a number or a date into a formatted string. Here are a few examples for dates. Important! The result of the TEXT function is text and not a date. You cannot do further date manipulation of the Calculated Column result from another Calculated Column.

Assuming yourDateColumn contains 4/1/2017 8:15 AM:

=TEXT(yourDateColumn,"yyyy")	2017
=TEXT(yourDateColumn,"M")	4
=TEXT(yourDateColumn,"MM")	04
=TEXT(yourDateColumn,"MMM")	Apr
=TEXT(yourDateColumn,"MMMM")	April
=TEXT(yourDateColumn,"d")	1
=TEXT(yourDateColumn,"dd")	01
=TEXT(yourDateColumn,"ddd")	Sat
=TEXT(yourDateColumn,"dddd")	Saturday
=TEXT(yourDateColumn,"dddd mmmm dd, yyyy")	Saturday April 01, 2017

The format strings, "yyyy" for example, are generally the same as the format strings used in the Excel.

Blank Dates

The TEXT function will treat blank dates as 12/30/1899, so you will want to wrap the TEXT function inside of an ISBLANK function.

Fiscal Year

If a fiscal year ends June 30th, and you refer to July 1st 2018 as the first fiscal day of 2018 and June 30th 2019 as the last fiscal day of 2018, then the following formula will return the fiscal year number. If July 1st 2018 is the start of fiscal year 2019, then add 1 to each of the following formulas. And of course, adjust the "6" and the "30" in the formulas to match the last day of your fiscal year.

```
=IF( [SomeDate] <= DATE(YEAR([SomeDate]), 6, 30),
     YEAR([SomeDate])-1, YEAR([SomeDate]) )
```

The above can be mathematically simplified a bit:

```
=YEAR([SomeDate]) - IF([SomeDate] <= DATE( YEAR([SomeDate]), 6, 30), 1, 0 )
```

If you want to make it prettier, just add " "FY "& " in front of either formula.

```
="FY " & YEAR([SomeDate]) - IF([SomeDate] <= DATE( YEAR([SomeDate]),6,30), 1, 0)
```

And if there is a chance of a blank date then add a ISBLANK test:

```
=IF( ISBLANK([SomeDate]), "",
     "FY " & YEAR([SomeDate]) - IF([SomeDate] <= DATE(YEAR([SomeDate]), 6, 30), 1, 0) )
```

Week Number

As the handy Excel WEEKNUM() function is not supported by SharePoint, we need to find a workaround. The definition of a week number varies by company, government and culture. Here we will focus on emulating the Excel WEEKNUM function. WEEKNUM in Excel has an optional parameter to select a "return type" to select how weeks are counted.

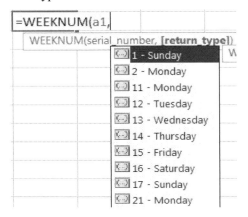

Not obvious from that dropdown list of return types, but there are two categories of return types that Excel calls "system 1" and "system 2". System 2 is based on the ISO 8601 standard commonly used in Europe.

- Category 1: Week 1 is the first week containing January 1st.
  - o By default, weeks start on a Sunday.
  - o You can select the first day of a week by adding a "return_type" parameter.
    - 1 and 17 are both Sunday
    - 2 and 11 are both Monday
    - 11 to 17 are Monday to Sunday
- Category 2: Week 1 is the first week containing a Thursday.
  - o The ISO 8601 standard.
  - o "return_type" 21 is the only category 2 type.
  - o Week 1 is the first week of the year starting on or after a Monday and includes Thursday.
  - o The week always starts on a Monday. (Sunday is part of the previous week.)

Week number examples:

Day	Date	return type 1	2	11	12	14	21		Day	Date	return type 1	2	11	12	14	21
Friday	12/30/2016	53	53	53	53	53	52		Sunday	12/30/2018	53	52	52	53	53	52
Saturday	12/31/2016	53	53	53	53	53	52		Monday	12/31/2018	53	53	53	53	53	1
Sunday	1/01/2017	1	1	1	1	1	52		Tuesday	1/01/2019	1	1	1	1	1	1
Monday	1/02/2017	1	2	2	1	1	1		Wednesday	1/02/2019	1	1	1	1	1	1
Tuesday	1/03/2017	1	2	2	2	1	1		Thursday	1/03/2019	1	1	1	1	2	1
Wednesday	1/04/2017	1	2	2	2	1	1		Friday	1/04/2019	1	1	1	1	2	1
Thursday	1/05/2017	1	2	2	2	2	1		Saturday	1/05/2019	1	1	1	1	2	1
Friday	1/06/2017	1	2	2	2	2	1		Sunday	1/06/2019	2	1	1	1	2	1
Saturday	1/07/2017	1	2	2	2	2	1		Monday	1/07/2019	2	2	2	1	2	2
Sunday	1/08/2017	2	2	2	2	2	1		Tuesday	1/08/2019	2	2	2	2	2	2
Monday	1/09/2017	2	3	3	2	2	2		Wednesday	1/09/2019	2	2	2	2	2	2
Tuesday	1/10/2017	2	3	3	3	2	2		Thursday	1/10/2019	2	2	2	2	3	2
Wednesday	1/11/2017	2	3	3	3	2	2		Friday	1/11/2019	2	2	2	2	3	2
Thursday	1/12/2017	2	3	3	3	3	2		Saturday	1/12/2019	2	2	2	2	3	2
Friday	1/13/2017	2	3	3	3	3	2		Sunday	1/13/2019	3	2	2	2	3	2
Saturday	1/14/2017	2	3	3	3	3	2		Monday	1/14/2019	3	3	3	2	3	3
Saturday	12/30/2017	52	53	53	53	53	52		Monday	12/30/2019	53	53	53	52	53	1
Sunday	12/31/2017	53	53	53	53	53	52		Tuesday	12/31/2019	53	53	53	53	53	1
Monday	1/01/2018	1	1	1	1	1	1		Wednesday	1/01/2020	1	1	1	1	1	1
Tuesday	1/02/2018	1	1	1	2	1	1		Thursday	1/02/2020	1	1	1	1	2	1
Wednesday	1/03/2018	1	1	1	2	1	1		Friday	1/03/2020	1	1	1	1	2	1
Thursday	1/04/2018	1	1	1	2	2	1		Saturday	1/04/2020	1	1	1	1	2	1
Friday	1/05/2018	1	1	1	2	2	1		Sunday	1/05/2020	2	1	1	1	2	1
Saturday	1/06/2018	1	1	1	2	2	1		Monday	1/06/2020	2	2	2	1	2	2
Sunday	1/07/2018	2	1	1	2	2	1		Tuesday	1/07/2020	2	2	2	2	2	2
Monday	1/08/2018	2	2	2	2	2	2		Wednesday	1/08/2020	2	2	2	2	2	2
Tuesday	1/09/2018	2	2	2	3	2	2		Thursday	1/09/2020	2	2	2	2	3	2
Wednesday	1/10/2018	2	2	2	3	2	2		Friday	1/10/2020	2	2	2	2	3	2
Thursday	1/11/2018	2	2	2	3	3	2		Saturday	1/11/2020	2	2	2	2	3	2
Friday	1/12/2018	2	2	2	3	3	2		Sunday	1/12/2020	3	2	2	2	3	2
Saturday	1/13/2018	2	2	2	3	3	2		Monday	1/13/2020	3	3	3	2	3	3
Sunday	1/14/2018	3	2	2	3	3	2		Tuesday	1/14/2020	3	3	3	3	3	3

Note: In all of the formula examples that follow, if your date columns include times, wrap each column name in an INT function to round to the nearest day. I.e. INT([*SomeDate*])

Return Type 1 or 17 – Category 1, Week starts on a Sunday

This formula has two parts: an adjustment for the first weekday of the year, and a rounded divide by 7 to get the number of weeks from the start of the year.

```
=INT( ( [SomeDate] - DATE( YEAR([SomeDate]), 1, 1 ) + 7
     - WEEKDAY( [SomeDate], 1 )
     ) / 7 ) + 1
```

Return Type 2 or 11 – Category 1, Week starts on a Monday

This formula is almost identical to the Type 1 formula, with an adjustment for the day of the week. Note the "-1" in the WEEKDAY function.

```
=INT( ( [SomeDate] - DATE( YEAR([SomeDate]), 1, 1 ) + 7
     - WEEKDAY( [SomeDate] - 1, 1 )
   ) / 7 ) + 1
```

Return Types 11-17 – Category 1, Week starts on a Monday-Sunday

As noted for the Type 2 example above, we only need an adjustment for the starting day of the week. Simply replace the -1 in the above example with one of the following values:

- Type 11, week starts on a Monday: -1
- Type 12, week starts on a Tuesday: -2
- Type 13, week starts on a Wednesday: -3
- Type 14, week starts on a Thursday: -4
- Type 15, week starts on a Friday: -5
- Type 16, week starts on a Saturday: -6
- Type 17, week starts on a Sunday: -0 (or leave it out)

For weeks that start on a Wednesday, we need Return Type 13, or a "-3".

```
=INT( ( [SomeDate] - DATE( YEAR([SomeDate]), 1, 1 ) + 7
     - WEEKDAY( [SomeDate] - 1, 1 )
   ) / 7 ) + 1
```

Displaying the Week Number as YYYY-WW

You may want to format the week number for better display and sorting by displaying the year and then the week number. The following will display something like: 2018-01

```
=YEAR( [SomeDate] ) & "-" & RIGHT( "0" & yourWeekNumberFormulaHere , 2 )
```

Return Type 21 – Category 2 (ISO 8601), Week starts on a Monday

This formula depends on the fact that dates are numbers starting from a "zero date", which for Excel and SharePoint is 1/1/1900, and is a Sunday. You can then take this number, divide it by 7, and round the results using INT, to get the number of full weeks from the "zero date". Adjust the calculation to insure that week 1 of a year includes a Thursday, and you get the week number.

While there are a number of solutions on the web, and they work in the limited timeframe of their examples, they don't always produce the same results as the Excel WEEKNUM(date, 21) function. The formula below has been tested out to 2050 with no differences from the Excel function.

=INT(

   ([*SomeDate*] - (DATE(YEAR([*SomeDate*] - WEEKDAY([*SomeDate*], 2) + 4), 1, 1) + 2)

   +WEEKDAY(DATE(YEAR([*SomeDate*] - WEEKDAY([*SomeDate*], 2) + 4), 1, 1) + 2) + 5)

   /7)

How it works:

Get January 1st of the ISO week year:

DATE(YEAR([*SomeDate*]-WEEKDAY([*SomeDate*], 2) + 4), 1, 1)

Calculate an offset to deal with finding the first week with a Thursday: (This number is the same for the entire year.)

[*SomeDate*] - (DATE(YEAR([*SomeDate*] - WEEKDAY([*SomeDate*], 2) + 4), 1, 1) + 2)

Add an integer divide (round down) by 7 to get the week number:

=INT(

   ([*SomeDate*] - (DATE(YEAR([*SomeDate*] - WEEKDAY([*SomeDate*], 2) + 4), 1, 1) + 2)

   + WEEKDAY(DATE(YEAR([*SomeDate*] - WEEKDAY([*SomeDate*], 2) + 4), 1, 1) + 2) + 5)

   /7)

To display the ISO year and the week number:

=YEAR([SomeDate] - WEEKDAY([SomeDate], 2) + 4) & " − " & RIGHT("00" &
INT(

   ([*SomeDate*] - (DATE(YEAR([*SomeDate*] - WEEKDAY([*SomeDate*], 2) + 4), 1, 1) + 2)

   + WEEKDAY(DATE(YEAR([*SomeDate*] - WEEKDAY([*SomeDate*],2) + 4), 1, 1) + 2) + 5)

   /7)
,2)

Day of the Year

This simple formula just returns the day of the year. January 1st is day 1, etc. It takes a date and then subtracts the first of the year.

=[SomeDate] - DATE(YEAR([SomeDate]), 1, 1) + 1

If you would like to display it in the form of 2018-123 then:

```
=YEAR( [SomeDate] ) & "-" &
 RIGHT( "00" & ( [SomeDate] - DATE( YEAR( [SomeDate] ), 1, 1 ) + 1 ), 3 )
```

And if there might be blank dates:

```
=IF( ISBLANK( [SomeDate] ), "",
    YEAR( [SomeDate] ) & "-" &
    RIGHT( "00" & ( [SomeDate] - DATE( YEAR( [SomeDate] ), 1, 1 ) + 1 ), 3 )
    )
```

First Day of the Current Month

Here are two techniques to get the first day of the month. One involves a calculation, and the other creates a new date from the month and year of a date.

A Little Calculation

We can use the DAY() function to return the day of month portion of a date. The DAY() of "12/14/2017" is 14. Subtract this number from the date and you get the last day of the previous month, but if you add 1 back then you get the first day of the month. To find the first of the month for a column named "SomeDate":

```
= [SomeDate] - DAY( [SomeDate] ) + 1
```

Build a New Date

The DATE() function lets you build a date from numeric values for the year, month and day. To build "12/14/2017" use DATE(2017,12,14). So, to get the first day of the month for a column named "SomeDate" build a new date using the year and month of the date:

```
=DATE( YEAR( [SomeDate] ), MONTH( [SomeDate] ), 1 )
```

The "1" at the end is for the day.

First Day of the Next Month

For this one, just use the DATE() function and add one to the month. Set the year to the column's year, the month to the column's month plus one, and set the day to the first of the month.

```
=DATE( YEAR( [SomeDate] ), MONTH( [SomeDate] ) + 1, 1 )
```

What about December? Turns out that the DATE() function can deal with months greater than 12. It just adjusts the year. As an example, DATE(2017,13,1) creates January 1st of 2018.

Last Day of the Current Month

Just get the first day of the next month and subtract 1!

=DATE(YEAR([SomeDate]), MONTH([SomeDate]) + 1, 1) **- 1**

Last Day of the Previous Month

The first example above for the "first day of the month" actually creates the "last day of the previous month", if you don't add the 1.

= [SomeDate] - DAY([SomeDate])

You could also use the DATE() function example we used above and just subtract 1. I.e., just get the first of the current month, and then subtract one.

=DATE(YEAR([SomeDate]), MONTH([SomeDate]), 1) - 1

Last Day of the Next Month

Having seen the previous samples, this one should be easy to figure out. Use the DATE() function and just add two the month, set the day to 1 and then subtract 1 from the calculated date.

=DATE(YEAR([SomeDate]), MONTH([SomeDate]) + **2**, 1) **-1**

Third Tuesday of a Month

We often need to schedule a task review, or a meeting, based some rule like "the fourth Thursday of each month". The algorithms in the examples below basically calculate the first day of the current month, the day of the week of the first day of the current month, and then the offset to get to the Nth weekday of the month.

The Nth Day of the Week in the Current Month

Two magic numbers in the formula:

- The target day of the week: 1=Sunday, 2=Tuesday, … 7=Saturday
- Nth week as: (nth_week -1) * 7   Example: 4th week would be 3 * 7, or 21

For the 4th Thursday (so 5 for Thursday and 21 for the 4th week) for a date column named "SomeDate":

```
=DATE( YEAR(SomeDate),MONTH(SomeDate),1 )
  + 5 - WEEKDAY( DATE( YEAR(SomeDate),MONTH(SomeDate),1 ) )
  + 21
  + IF( WEEKDAY( DATE( YEAR(SomeDate),MONTH(SomeDate),1 ) ) > 5, 7, 0)
```

The result looks like this:

SomeDate ↑	NthDateOfMonth	DayOfWeek
5/1/2018	5/24/2018	Thursday
5/24/2018	5/24/2018	Thursday
5/25/2018	5/24/2018	Thursday
5/31/2018	5/24/2018	Thursday
6/1/2018	6/28/2018	Thursday
7/1/2018	7/26/2018	Thursday

For the 1st Monday (so 2 for Monday and 0 for the 1st week) for a date column named "SomeDate":

```
=DATE( YEAR(SomeDate),MONTH(SomeDate),1)
  + 2 - WEEKDAY( DATE( YEAR(SomeDate),MONTH(SomeDate),1 ) )
  + 0
  + IF( WEEKDAY( DATE( YEAR(SomeDate),MONTH(SomeDate),1 ) ) > 2, 7, 0)
```

You of course can leave off the "+ 0"!

Here are the parts of the formula:

Get the date of the first day of the month. (for 1/5/2018 that would be 1/1/2018)

```
=DATE( YEAR(SomeDate),MONTH(SomeDate),1)
```

Add to that the day of week number (5 for Thursday) minus the day of week number for the first of the month. (Yup, we have to calculate that twice!)

Get the offset from the first day of the week to the first Thursday:

```
  + 5 - WEEKDAY( DATE( YEAR(SomeDate),MONTH(SomeDate),1 ) )
```

And then adjust "x" number of weeks into the month: (using (week -1) * 7)

```
  + 21
```

And finally, what if the first day of the month is after the target date? The first Thursday is in the second week of the month, not the first! So, add seven more days.

```
  + IF( WEEKDAY( DATE( YEAR(SomeDate),MONTH(SomeDate),1 ) ) > 5, 7, 0)
```

The Nth Day of the Week in the Month, but always in the future.

The previous example always returned a date in the current month, even if it was in the past. If we need the Nth day of week of a future date, then things get a little more complicated. We need to check the "4th Thursday" to make sure it is in the future, if so display that date, or add one to the month (Month(SomeDate)+1) and repeat the calculation.

```
=IF(
  DATE( YEAR(SomeDate),MONTH(SomeDate),1 )
    +  5 - WEEKDAY( DATE( YEAR(SomeDate),MONTH(SomeDate),1 ) )
    +  21
    +  IF( WEEKDAY( DATE( YEAR(SomeDate),MONTH(SomeDate),1 )) >5, 7, 0)
    > SomeDate,

  DATE( YEAR(SomeDate),MONTH(SomeDate),1 )
    +  5 - WEEKDAY( DATE( YEAR(SomeDate),MONTH(SomeDate),1 ) )
    +  21
    +  IF( WEEKDAY( DATE( YEAR(SomeDate),MONTH(SomeDate),1 ))> 5, 7, 0),

  DATE( YEAR(SomeDate),MONTH(SomeDate)+1, 1 )
    +  5 - WEEKDAY( DATE( YEAR(SomeDate),MONTH(SomeDate)+1, 1 ) )
    +  21
    +  IF( WEEKDAY( DATE( YEAR(SomeDate),MONTH(SomeDate)+1, 1 ))>5,7,0)
)
```

SomeDate	NthDayOfMonthFuture	DayOfWeek2
5/1/2018	5/24/2018	Thursday
5/24/2018	6/28/2018	Thursday
5/25/2018	6/28/2018	Thursday
5/31/2018	6/28/2018	Thursday
6/1/2018	6/28/2018	Thursday
7/1/2018	7/26/2018	Thursday

Almost looks like we are going to wear out the **SomeDate** column! To adapt the above formula to your "Nth day of the month", replace:

- The 5 with your target day of the week: 1=Sunday, 2=Tuesday, … 7=Saturday
- The 21 with the value for your Nth week as: (week -1) * 7   Example: 3rd week would be 14

Do not replace the 0's, 1's or 7's in the sample formula.

Skipping Weekend Days

We often need to calculate a future date that is not a weekend day. For example, some event must be scheduled 3 days in the future, but not on a weekend. If the "trigger" date is on a Monday, then the event would be scheduled on Thursday. If the trigger date is a Thursday, we need to skip past Sunday and schedule the event on Monday.

Excel has a WORKDAY() function that can easily do this, but WORKDAY is not available for SharePoint Calculated Columns.

Next Workday "X" Days in the Future

If you are calculating a future date, and just need to make sure that it is not on a weekend day, just do a test for Saturday and for Sunday and add two or one to the date.

Assuming two columns named Start Date and Days, and a Calculated Column formatted as a date:

```
=[Start Date] + [Days] -1
  + IF( WEEKDAY( [Start Date] + [Days] - 1, 2) = 6, 2, 0)    adjust for Saturday
  + IF( WEEKDAY( [Start Date] + [Days] - 1, 2) = 7, 1, 0)    adjust for Sunday
```

Simple Solutions for 5, 10, 15 Working Days in the Future

If the start date is always on a weekday, and the future date is always a multiple of five days in the future, just add seven days for each five days!

Five working days in the future:

```
=[Start Date] + 7
```

Or a more general solution, but it works only when Work Days is a multiple of five:

```
=[Start Date] + [Work Days] / 5 * 7
```

Solution for Any Number of Working Days in the Future

I came up with a solution for this, but it was longer than I liked and not real clear, but it worked! I gave the challenge to my son Eric and he came up with a much shorter version, which is the one below.

This example assumes two columns, [Start Date] and [Working Days], and that "one working day" starts and ends on the same day.

=[Start Date] + [Working Days]

+ IF(WEEKDAY([Start Date], 3) < 5,

1 + FLOOR(([Working Days] - 6 + WEEKDAY([Start Date], 3)) / 5, 1) * 2,

7 - WEEKDAY([Start Date], 2) + FLOOR(([Working Days] - 1) / 5, 1) * 2

)

Here's a breakdown of the formula:

=[Start Date] + [Working Days]   *Start by just adding the days to the Start Date.*

+ IF(WEEKDAY([Start Date], 2) < 6,   *Is the Start Date a week day? (i.e. not Saturday or Sunday)*

Starts on a weekday, so calculate the number of weeks, multiply by 2 for number of weekend days
FLOOR is a round down function. WEEKDAY(x,2) returns a 1 form Monday and a 7 for Sunday.
1 + FLOOR(*round down*

([Working Days] - 7   *subtract the days from the first week*

+ WEEKDAY([Start Date], 2)) / 5, 1)   *divide total days by 5 for the number of weeks*

* 2,   *multiple by 2 for 2 day weekends*

Else, starts on a weekend,

7 - WEEKDAY([Start Date], 2)   *adjust from weekend to the first Monday*

+ FLOOR(*round down*

([Working Days] - 1) / 5, 1)   *divide total days by 5 for the number of weeks*

* 2,   *multiple by 2 for 2 day weekends*

)

The above formula can be reordered to slightly shorten it, but the original is probably easier to figure out.

=[Start Date]+[Working Days]
  + 1
  + 2 * FLOOR(([Working Days]
                + IF(WEEKDAY([Start Date], 2) = 7, -1, 0) - 7
                + WEEKDAY([Start Date], 2)) / 5, 1)
  + IF(WEEKDAY([Start Date], 2) = 7, -1, 0)

Number of Working Days Between Two Dates

The following formula calculates the number of working days (M-F) between two weekday dates. There are two assumptions: The date values are Dates and not Date and Time, and the date values are Monday to Friday only.

```
=[Due Date] - [Start Date] + 1 -

IF( [Due Date] < ( [Start Date] + ( 5 - WEEKDAY([Start Date],3) ) ),

    0,

    FLOOR(  ( ([Due Date]-([Start Date]+(5-WEEKDAY([Start Date],3)))) /7),1)*2 + 2

)
```

The first line is all that is needed if both dates are in the same week.

The rest of the formula tests to see if the both dates are in the same week, and if so, makes no adjustment (0), otherwise deducts two days for each weekend between the two dates.

Reminder:

- This formula does not allow for when start or end date is a weekend date. You could add extra logic to test for this.
- Add validation to the two date columns to require M-F dates and that the start date must be before the end date!

Number of Working Hours Between Two Dates

If you need the number of working hours between a start date and time and an end date and time, then you will need to write a formula that can skip weekend days.

To find working hours excluding weekends and assuming a work day from 8AM to 5PM (9 hours) then:

```
=( INT([Due Date]) - INT([Start Date]) + 1 ) * 9

  - IF( INT([Due Date]) < (INT([Start Date]) + ( 5 - WEEKDAY([Start Date],3) ) ),

      0,

      FLOOR( ( ( INT([Due Date]) - ( INT([Start Date]) + ( 5 - WEEKDAY([Start Date], 3 ) ) ) ) / 7
              ), 1) * 2 * 9 + 2 * 9

    )

  -((([Start Date]-INT([Start Date]))*24-8)
```

94

-(17-([Due Date]-INT([Due Date]))*24)

This assumes all entries are M-F and between the hours of 9 and 5. It does not work correctly for weekend dates or hours outside of 9 to 5.

Here's an example of the results:

Start Date	Due Date	Working Hours (9)
5/1/2018 8:00 AM	5/4/2018 5:00 PM	36.00
5/1/2018 8:00 AM	5/7/2018 5:00 PM	45.00
5/1/2018 8:00 AM	5/8/2018 5:00 PM	54.00
5/1/2018 8:00 AM	5/14/2018 5:00 PM	90.00
5/1/2018 8:00 AM	5/28/2018 5:00 PM	180.00
5/1/2018 8:00 AM	5/4/2018 4:00 PM	35.00
5/1/2018 8:00 AM	5/4/2018 3:30 PM	34.50
5/1/2018 8:00 AM	5/1/2018 11:00 AM	3.00

To find working hours excluding weekends and assuming a work day from 9AM to 5PM (8 hours) then:

=(INT([Due Date])-INT([Start Date])+1) * 8

  - IF(INT([Due Date]) < (INT([Start Date]) + (5 - WEEKDAY([Start Date],3))),

    0,

    FLOOR(((INT([Due Date]) - (INT([Start Date]) + (5 - WEEKDAY([Start Date], 3)))) / 7
        ), 1) * 2 * 8 + 2 * 8

)

  -(([Start Date]-INT([Start Date]))*24-9)

  -(17-([Due Date]-INT([Due Date]))*24)

How it works:

The first line calculates the number of hours based on each day being a full eight hours and that weekends are also working days.

=(INT([Due Date]) - INT([Start Date]) + 1) * 8

This checks to see if the start date and end date are both in the same week.

- IF(INT([Due Date]) < (INT([Start Date]) + (5 - WEEKDAY([Start Date],3))),

If in the same week, no weekend adjustments are needed.

0,

If not in the same week, then we need to subtract the number of weekends, multiplied by two to get the days per weekend, and then multiplied by eight for the working hours per day.

FLOOR(((INT([Due Date]) - (INT([Start Date]) + (5 - WEEKDAY([Start Date], 3)))) / 7), 1) * 2 * 8 + 2 * 8

Adjust for when then first day does not start at 9 AM.

-(([Start Date] - INT([Start Date])) * 24 - 9)

Adjust for when then last day does not end at 5 PM (1700 hours).

- (17 - ([Due Date] - INT([Due Date])) * 24)

To adjust this formula for other times:

- Change the "24 - 9" to "24 - yourStartingTime".
- Change "17" to your ending time (24 hour clock – 17 = 5:00 PM)
- Change the "8" values to the total number of hours per day.

Formatting Numbers

You will usually use the built-in features to format numbers in Calculated Columns.

The data type returned from this formula is:

○ Single line of text

○ Number (1, 1.0, 100)

◉ Currency ($, ¥, €)

○ Date and Time

○ Yes/No

Number of decimal places:

| Automatic ▾ |

Currency format:

| $123,456.00 (United States)   ▾ |

When these options do not meet your needs, you can use the TEXT() function to create custom formats using Excel-style formatting strings.

The general pattern is:

=TEXT([Column to format], "*format*")

=TEXT([Column to format], "*positiveFormat*; *negativeFormat* ")

=TEXT([Column to format], "*positiveFormat*; *negativeFormat*; *zeroFormat*;")

Here's an example for a SharePoint column named "SomeNumber":

=TEXT([SomeNumber], "#,##0;(#,##0);""""zero"""")

See the next section for why some of the quotes are doubled.

12,345	12,345
-1,000	(1,000)
0	zero

Tip: Set the Calculated Column's result format to Number to right align the values.

12,345
(1,000)
zero

The data type returned from this formula is:

○ Single line of text

◉ Number (1, 1.0, 100)

Adding Text to Numbers

The Excel TEXT function documentation shows how to merge text into the format..

$0.00" Surplus";$-0.00" Shortage"

Those quotes (") can be a problem unless you know a little trick… double any embedded quotes! In the following example we are formatting a column named "SomeNumber" with some text to explain what the positive and negative numbers mean. Note where the Excel example had a quote (") we have replaced them with two quotes ("").

=TEXT([SomeNumber], "$0.00"" Surplus"";$-0.00"" Shortage""")

The result looks like this:

SomeNumber	TEXT()
1,000	$1000.00 Surplus
3,999	$3999.00 Surplus
-1,000	$-1000.00 Shortage

Adding Special Symbols (¥, £, etc.) to TEXT() Number Formats

The Excel TEXT function documentation shows how you can just add special symbols like ¥ to a format.

=TEXT(A1,"¥0.00")

If you try adding ¥ to a TEXT function in SharePoint you will get the "#VALUE!" error. In a SharePoint Calculated Column you will need to use double quotes around the symbol, in addition to any other needed quotes.

=TEXT([SomeNumber], """¥"""0.00")

Note that some characters are not supported in all fonts or in all browsers.

Tip! If you know the ASCII code for a symbol, you can enter it by holding the ALT key and typing the four digits on the numeric keypad.

Examples:

¢ ALT+0162
£ ALT+0163
¥ ALT+0165
€ ALT+0128

You can use the Windows Character Map utility to enter the symbols or find the codes.

Converting Numbers to Fractions

Note: Read to the end to see a shorter version that uses CHOOSE instead of nested IFs.

In Excel you can get fractions using TEXT(yourNumberColumn,"# ?/?"):

4	4
4.1	4
4.12	4 1/8
4.125	4 1/8
4.5	4 1/2
4.75	4 3/4

The same function in SharePoint will round down number, and for each of the above examples, return 4. If you need fractions, then you will need to write your own function to create them. Below we have several versions of this function.

Value	Fractions	w Symbols
4.25	4 1/4	4 ¼
12	12	12
4.75	4 3/4	4 ¾
4.333	4 1/4	4 ¼
4.999	5	5
4.8	4 3/4	4 ¾

Function to return the fractions 0, 1/4, 1/2, and 3/4

```
=IF( yourNumberColumn - INT(yourNumberColumn) = 0.25,
        INT( yourNumberColumn) & " 1/4",
    IF( yourNumberColumn - INT(yourNumberColumn) = 0.5,
        INT( yourNumberColumn) & " 1/2",
      IF ( yourNumberColumn - INT(yourNumberColumn) = 0.75,
          INT( yourNumberColumn) & " 3/4",
            INT(yourNumberColumn) ) ) )
```

If you need your function to round off to the nearest 1/4th, replace the first value in each IF with:

```
ROUND( yourNumberColumn * 4, 0 ) / 4
```

to get this formula:

```
=IF( ROUND( yourNumberColumn*4, 0 ) / 4 -INT(yourNumberColumn) = 0.25,
    INT(yourNumberColumn) & " 1/4",
  IF( ROUND(yourNumberColumn * 4, 0 ) / 4 - INT(yourNumberColumn) = 0.5,
    INT(yourNumberColumn) & " 1/2",
   IF( ROUND(yourNumberColumn * 4 , 0 ) / 4 - INT(yourNumberColumn) = 0.75,
    INT( yourNumberColumn) & " 3/4",
      ROUND( yourNumberColumn,0) ) ) )
```

If you would like to see ¼ instead of 1/4 then use the CHAR function to get those symbols. While the ¼, ½, and ¾ characters are available, 1/3 and 1/8 are not.

- Replace " 1/4" with " " & CHAR(188)

- Replace " 1/2" with " " & CHAR(189)
- Replace " 3/4" with " " & CHAR(190)

```
=IF( ROUND( yourNumberColumn * 4, 0 ) / 4 -INT(yourNumberColumn) = 0.25,
    INT(yourNumberColumn) & " " & CHAR(188),
  IF( ROUND(yourNumberColumn * 4, 0 ) / 4 - INT(yourNumberColumn) = 0.5,
    INT(yourNumberColumn) & " " & CHAR(189),
  IF( ROUND(yourNumberColumn * 4, 0 ) / 4 -INT(yourNumberColumn)=0.75,
    INT( yourNumberColumn) & " " & CHAR(190),
    ROUND( yourNumberColumn, 0 ) ) ) )
```

Function to return the fractions 0, 1/8, 1/4, 3/8, 1/2, 5/8, 3/4, and 7/8

To add support for eighths we need to add four more IFs. If we change the number used in our rounding code from 4 to 8, and add a few lines, then we can display values to the nearest eighth.

```
=IF( ROUND(yourNumberColumn * 8, 0 ) / 8 - INT(yourNumberColumn) = 0.125,
        INT(yourNumberColumn) & " 1/8",
    IF( ROUND(yourNumberColumn * 8, 0 ) / 8 - INT(yourNumberColumn) = 0.25,
        INT(yourNumberColumn) & " 1/4",
    IF( ROUND(yourNumberColumn * 8, 0 ) / 8 - INT(yourNumberColumn) = 0.375,
        INT(yourNumberColumn) & " 3/8",
    IF( ROUND(yourNumberColumn * 8, 0 ) / 8 - INT(yourNumberColumn) = 0.5,
        INT(yourNumberColumn) & " 1/2",
    IF( ROUND(yourNumberColumn * 8, 0 ) / 8 - INT(yourNumberColumn) = 0.625,
        INT(yourNumberColumn) & " 5/8",
    IF( ROUND(yourNumberColumn * 8, 0 ) / 8 - INT(yourNumberColumn) = 0.75,
        INT(yourNumberColumn) & " 3/4",
    IF( ROUND(yourNumberColumn * 8, 0 ) / 8 - INT(yourNumberColumn) = 0.875,
        INT(yourNumberColumn) & " 7/8",
    ROUND(yourNumberColumn, 0 ) ) ) ) ) ) ) )
```

Now we have fractions to the nearest 1/8th.

4.125	4 1/8
4.25	4 1/4
4.5	4 1/2
4.625	4 5/8
4.75	4 3/4
4.875	4 7/8
4.88	4 7/8
5	5

A Much Shorter Version that uses CHOOSE

Here is a much shorter version of a formula to display a number as a fraction:

```
=ROUNDDOWN( yourNumberColumn + 0.062499, 0 ) &
   CHOOSE( ( ROUND( yourNumberColumn * 8, 0 ) / 8 - INT(yourNumberColumn) ) * 8 + 1,
              ""," 1/8"," 1/4"," 3/8"," 1/2", " 5/8", " 3/4", " 7/8",""
            )
```

This uses the CHOOSE function to pick the text to display for "less than 1/8th", "1/8th" … "7/8th" and "more than 7/8th". (Nine possible values.) *(and it uses three difference rounding functions!)*

To get the fraction:

1. Round the number to the nearest 1/8th:
   ```
   ( ROUND( yourNumberColumn * 8, 0 ) / 8 - INT(yourNumberColumn) ) * 8
   ```
2. And as CHOOSE starts with 1 and not 0, add one to the result:
   ```
   ( ROUND( yourNumberColumn * 8, 0 ) / 8 - INT(yourNumberColumn) ) * 8 + 1
   ```
3. Use CHOOSE to pick the text:
   ```
   CHOOSE(  …   , ""," 1/8"," 1/4"," 3/8"," 1/2", " 5/8", " 3/4", " 7/8","")
   ```
4. Concatenate that to the rounded down number:
   ```
    ROUNDDOWN( yourNumberColumn + 0.062499, 0 ) & …
   ```
   The "+ 0.062499" is added to deal with the last 1/16th after "7/8th" so we round up to the next higher number.

Financial Calculations

You can use a many of the Excel financial functions in your Calculated columns. Not all functions are supported. For example, while DDB depreciation function is supported, the DB function is not. In general, functions that require ranges of cells (A1:A20), like IIR, will not work in SharePoint formulas. The NPV function will work, but only when supplied with a comma delimited list of values.

For a complete list see: https://support.office.com/en-us/article/Examples-of-common-formulas-in-SharePoint-Lists-d81f5f21-2b4e-45ce-b170-bf7ebf6988b3

Here are a few of the supported functions:

- NPV – Net Present Value
- PMT – Payment
- PPMT – Principal paid on n[th] payment
- NPER – Number of Periods (based on constant payments and interest rate)

Calculating Payments

If you need a payment function, you might first create and test it in Excel.

1. Name a cell with the same name as your column, "Price" in this example, and enter a test value. (See the "Tips for Formulas" chapter for Excel testing details.)

2. Write the formula.

=PMT(8%/12, 36, Price)

PMT(**rate**, nper, pv, [fv], [type])

3. You will probably want to add a minus sign so the payment is displayed as a positive number.

=-PMT(8%/12, 36, Price)

PMT(**rate**, nper, pv, [fv], [type])

4. Enter a few prices to test the formula.

5. Then copy it to SharePoint (after adding square brackets and spaces in column names where needed):

Formula:

=-PMT(8%/12, 36, Price)

Insert Column:

Car
Created
Modified
Pmt 48 mths
Price

Add to formula

The data type returned from this formula is:

○ Single line of text

○ Number (1, 1.0, 100)

◉ Currency ($, ¥, €)

6. Test!

Car		Price	Pmt 36 mths	Pmt 48 mths
Vega ✳	•••	$2,090	$65.49	$51.02
Pinto ✳	•••	$1,850	$57.97	$45.16
Corvette ✳	•••	$59,000	$1,848.85	$1,440.36

Amount Applied to Principle (PPMT)

While PMT can tell you the loan payment amount, PPMT can tell you how much of the payment is for the principal for any one period. In this example we want to list the amount of the payment that applies to the principal for the 1st and the 36th payment.

Car		Price	Pmt 36 mths	Principal from 1st payment	Principal from 36th payment
Vega ☼	...	$2,090	$65.49	$51.56	$65.06
Pinto ☼	...	$1,850	$57.97	$45.64	$57.59
Corvette ☼	...	$59,000	$1,848.85	$1,455.51	$1,836.60

The formula for the 1st month:

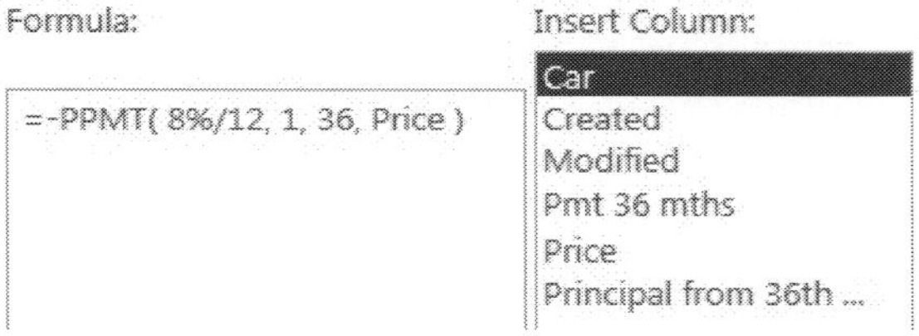

The Excel documentation:
https://support.office.com/en-us/article/PPMT-function-C370D9E3-7749-4CA4-BEEA-B06C6AC95E1B

Creating Random Numbers (Using NOW)

The Excel RAND() and RANDBETWEEN() functions do not work in SharePoint formulas. Calculated columns do support the NOW() function, and with a trick or two it can be used to create a random number. NOW() returns a numeric value that represents the current date and time. If formatted as a Date, or Date and Time, then you will see the current date. But, if you format it as Single Line of Text you will see something like: 42,691.3977137731, or a few seconds later: 42,691.3983521875. The last number starts to look like a random number! And if accurate, it changes every .0000000001 of a day, or about every 0.00000864 seconds. Close enough for me.

Notes:

- These are not guaranteed to be mathematically pure random numbers!
- The values depend on the exact instant that an item is added to a list and will change with each edit. (But will not change with each view.)

Get a random number between 0 and 9

This one looks easy, just pull off the last digit from NOW()!

=RIGHT(NOW() ,1)

But.. there's one flaw with this… The last digit of a fractional value is never displayed with a zero! (I.e. you will never see .111111110 unless custom formatted.) So, we need to pull off the next to last digit!

=LEFT(RIGHT(NOW() ,2) ,1)

Here's an example with our "random" number on the left, and the Now() value on the right.

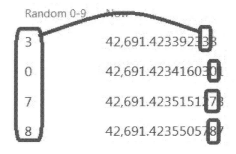

Get a random number between 0 and 999

If you need bigger numbers, just return more digits:

=RIGHT(NOW(),3)

As the RIGHT function creates a string (text), you may get leading zeros ("012"). To remove the leading zeros just do some math!

= 0 + RIGHT(NOW(),3)

Here are a few examples:

Random 0 - 999	Random 0-999 as num
546	546
449	449
356	356
708	708
398	398
741	741
044	44

But… (there's always a "but"), this will never return a value that ends with a zero. So… back to the LEFT function:

= 0 + **LEFT(** RIGHT(NOW(),4)**, 3)**

I.e. get the left three of the right four digits…

42,691.42081243006

Creating Random Messages (using CHOOSE)

I wanted to add a "motivational" message to a list of new sales. To be "fair", I wanted the messages to be random. (i.e. I did not want to think and create a good algorithm to pick an appropriate message!)

The result should look something like this:

✓	Title		Motivate
	Sale to IBM ✖	•••	Thanks!
	Sale to Microsoft ✖	•••	Good Job
	Sale to Apple ✖	•••	:-)
	Sale to HP ✖	•••	You are the MAX!
	Sale to Dell ✖	•••	Good Work
	Sale to General Electric ✖	•••	:-)
	Sale to Mike ✖	•••	You are the MAX!
	Sale to the city ✖	•••	Gold star for you!
	Sale to new customer ✖	•••	Wow!

All we need to do is combine the random number trick from the previous example with the CHOOSE function. As CHOOSE starts with item 1 and not item 0, we will need to add one to the random number.

Examples of a basic CHOOSE function:

=CHOOSE(1, "red", "green", "blue") will return "red".

=CHOOSE(3, "red", "green", "blue") will return "green".

Using numbers less than one and more than the number of items will return an error.

Here is the function to choose a random message:

```
=CHOOSE( LEFT( RIGHT( NOW() ,2), 1) + 1, "Good Job", "Wow!", "Good Work", "Thanks!",
   "Could be better", "Gold star for you!", "a free coffee for you!",":-)", "You are the MAX!",
   "Do it again!" )
```

Here's what it looks like in a Calculated Column:

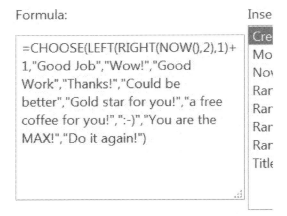

The data type returned from this formula is:

⦿ Single line of text

A Calculated Task Status

You can't always depend on users to set a Task status correctly. Here's a Calculated Column that always shows the correct status.

Rules for picking a status:

- No Start date or no Due date → "unscheduled"
- Start date is after Due date → "error"
- Has a Start date, has a Due Date and 100% Complete → "completed"
- Has a Start date and 0% Complete → "not started"
- Has a Start date, % Completed greater than 0% and less than 100% → "in progress"

The formula could be something like this:

```
=IF( OR( ISBLANK([Start Date]), ISBLANK([Due Date])), "Unscheduled",
   IF( [Start Date] > [Due Date], "Error",
      IF( [% Complete] = 1, "Completed",
```

```
    IF( [% Complete] = 0, "Not started",
     IF( AND( [% Complete] > 0, [% Complete] < 1 ), "In Progress",
      "Other"
) ) ) ) )
```

Notes:

- Although % Complete is displayed in a task list as 0% to 100%, internally it is stored as number from 0 to 1.
- The "Other" option is a "catch all" in case we missed a possible combination!

The result:

Task Name		Start Date	Due Date	% Complete	Work Status
Task 1	...	October 1, 2017	October 15, 2016	0 %	Error
Task 2	...			0 %	Unscheduled
Task 3	...	October 15, 2017	October 15, 2017	100 %	Completed
Task 4	...	October 2, 2017	October 12, 2017	50 %	In Progress
Task 5	...	October 1, 2017	October 15, 2017	100 %	Completed
Task 6	...	October 5, 2017	October 6, 2017	0 %	Not started
Task 7	...		October 20, 2017	0 %	Unscheduled
Task 8	...	October 4, 2017		0 %	Unscheduled

More notes:

- The one status you probably are looking for, "Past Due", is not possible as we cannot use the [Today] dynamic variable in SharePoint Calculated columns. But as SharePoint 2013, 2016,2019 and Online automatically displays the Due Date in red for past due tasks, we get the effect we need!
- SharePoint 2013's, 2016's and 2019's built-in status column is named "Task Status".
- SharePoint 2007's and 2010's built-in status column is named "Status".
- You can't detect "Unassigned" tasks in your formula as SharePoint Calculated columns cannot see "People and Group" columns. (You can use one of the workflow workarounds for this.)

Great Circle Distance from Longitude and Latitude

If you need to calculate the distance between two locations on a sphere, like the Earth, you use a formula to calculate the "great circle route" distance.

Notes:

- The formula below is from: http://bluemm.blogspot.com/2007/01/excel-formula-to-calculate-distance.html?m=1
- The formula below returns values in miles. For kilometers, change 6371 to 3958.756. For nautical miles use 3440.065. This number is the mean radius of the Earth.
- The longitude values are positive for East and negative for West. (Locations in the USA are West.)
- The SharePoint location column type introduced with SharePoint 2013 is not accessible by a Calculated Column.
- In this example, the Latitude1, Longitude1, Latitude2, Longitude2 columns are numeric columns.

```
=ACOS( COS( RADIANS(90-Latitude1) )
        * COS( RADIANS(90-Latitude2) )
        + SIN( RADIANS(90-Latitude1) )
        * SIN( RADIANS(90-Latitude2) )
        * COS( RADIANS(Longitude1-Longitude2) )
      ) * 6371
```

(Four trig functions in one example!)

Location1	Longitude1	Latitude1	Location2	Longitude2	Latitude2	Distance
Downtown Cincinnati	-84.511001	39.099901	Central Park NY	-73.965446	40.782772	570.12
Eiffel Tower, Kings Island	-84.26706	39.343308	Eiffel Tower, Paris	2.294327	48.858143	4,108.39

Simplify a Workflow by Using a Calculated Column

Some kinds logic that's easy to do in a Calculated Column can be difficult to duplicate in a workflow. Here are a few examples.

Example: Add a Calculated Column that decides if to send the email, and have the workflow test the Calculated Column

```
=IF( OR( [Status]=1, [Status]=2, [Status]=4 ), "Send an email", "no email for you" )
```

A side benefit of using a calculated column is that the rules for sending the email can be changed without editing the workflow, and the workflow is identical for multiple lists, even if the columns are not always the same.

Here's a formula that would only send the email if the list item was added on a weekend.

    =IF(WEEKDAY([Created], 2) >= 6 , "Send an email", "no email for you")

Note: A blank field is treated as a Saturday by WEEKDAY().

Ok, we have seen over 60 example formulas to get you started. If you come up with something really interesting, post it in a blog or one of the discussion forums!

5. Calculated Default Column Values

Many SharePoint columns have a Calculated Default option that at first glance looks like an interesting feature. Don't get your hopes up… you can't calculate a default ending date based on a start date column, or a default shipping cost based on product category. Bottom line, you can only do calculations based on the functions TODAY() and NOW().

Examples:

=[Today] + 5   If today is 2/1/18 then the default is 2/6/18

=TODAY() + 5   2/6/18

=NOW()   2/1/18 10:05 AM

=NOW() + 5.5   2/6/18 10:05 PM

=[ME]   *(not very useful… see below)*

About [ME]

The [ME] system variable returns the current user in an internal format:

- SharePoint Online: i:0#.f|membership|mike@somedomain.onmicrosoft.com
- SharePoint 2016 and 2019:   i:0#.w|yourDomain\mike

So depending on the version of SharePoint it will return information about how the user authenticated ("i:0#.w" = Windows authentication), and either their login name (domain\user) or their email. The [ME] variable might be useful in a People and Group column, but Calculated Defaults are not allowed there.

Calculated Defaults are only available for these column types:

- Single Line of Text
- Choice
- Number
- Currency
- Date and Time
- Task Outcome

Calculated Default Limitations

- Cannot use data from other columns.
- Pretty much limited to calculations using the current date and time. Examples:
    o Due Date: 7 days in the future
    o Year End
    o Last day of current month
- Limited to 355 characters.
- When the field is a required field, this feature does not work in Quick Edit view. But, does work as expected in the "New Item" form.

- When working with the Quick Edit view, the calculated default values are not displayed until you click off the line.

Also Consider

- You can set default values for columns for each folder using "Library Settings" > "Column default value settings". As an example, if you have one folder named "NE Region" you could set the default value for the "City" column to "Boston", and if you have another folder named "SE Region" you could set the default value for the "City" column to "Atlanta".
    o https://msdn.microsoft.com/en-us/library/office/ee557925(v=office.14).aspx

Examples

Default Date Due or Task End Date – 5 days in the Future

Calculated Defaults only work with the current date or date and time. While they cannot use dates from other columns, they can use the TODAY and NOW built-in variables.

=TODAY + 5

Default value:

   ○ (None)

   ○ Today's Date

   ○   [   ]   12 AM ▼   00 ▼

Enter date in M/D/YYYY format.

   ◉ Calculated Value:

   [=Today+5   ]

If you wanted the same day, a week in the future, use 7 instead of 5.

Default to X Days in the Future, but not a Weekend

In this default formula the number "4" is used for today plus 4 working days. Note that if you want to default to Thursday when today is Monday, use "3" instead of "4".

If today is 1/1/2018, a Monday, this will set the default to 1/5/2018, a Friday, but if today is 1/2/2018, a Tuesday, this will set the default to 1/8/2018 the next Monday.

```
=IF( WEEKDAY( TODAY+4, 3 ) = 5,    Is a Saturday

        TODAY+4+2,          Add two days to skip the weekend

    IF( WEEKDAY( TODAY+4, 3 ) = 6,    Is a Sunday

        TODAY+4+1,      Add one day to skip the weekend

        TODAY+4 ) )    Use the calculated date
```

This formula adds 4 to the current day, and then checks to see if the day is Saturday, and if so adds 2 days, or if the day is Sunday, adds 1 day.

First Day of the Current Month

To default to the first day of the current month, just calculate a new date using the DATE function and set the day to the first.

=DATE(YEAR(TODAY), MONTH(TODAY), 1)

First Day of the Next Month

Just use the previous formula and add one to the month.

=DATE(YEAR(TODAY), MONTH(TODAY), 1)

And it does work for December!   DATE(2018, 13, 1) returns "1/1/2019".

Last Day of the Current Month

Use the First Day of Next Month formula and subtract one to the date.

=DATE(YEAR(TODAY), MONTH(TODAY), 1) - 1

The Nth Day of the Week in the Current Month

This formula calculates the "the fourth Thursday of the month".

=DATE(YEAR(TODAY),MONTH(TODAY),1)

  + 5 - WEEKDAY(DATE(YEAR(TODAY),MONTH(TODAY),1))

  + 21

  + IF(WEEKDAY(DATE(YEAR(TODAY),MONTH(TODAY),1)) > 5, 7, 0)

See "The Nth Day of the Week in the Current Month" in the Calculated Column Examples chapter for the details on how this one works and how to change it to work with other "nth" days of the month.

The Nth Day of the Week in the Month, but always in the future.

We can't do this example from the Calculated Column Examples chapter due to the 355 character limit. (My formula is 413 characters long with every space removed!) Maybe you can find, and share, a way to do it!

Setting Default Text in a Single Line of Text Column

Remembering that we are limited to defaults based on today's date, you might preload a notes or comments column with some date based text. Note that this does not work for Multiple Lines of Text columns.

="Notes for "&TEXT(TODAY,"mm/dd/yyyy")

Default value:

○ Text   ⊙ Calculated Value

="Notes for "&TEXT(Today,

The "New" form with the default text:

Title *   Notes for 03/25/2018

6.   **Column Validation Formulas**

Column validation formulas are used to create custom validations for user entered data. These can be used to make sure that quantities are not negative and vacation requests are for dates in the future. These validations are limited to the current column only. They cannot use data from other columns. For validations across multiple columns use List / Library validation formulas. (See Chapter 8)

Column Validation Limitations

- Column Validations Cannot be Applied to All Column Types.
- Column Validation formulas have a maximum length of 1024 characters in all versions.
- Column Validation formulas can only "see" the current column. While "[Price] > 0" is a valid validation for the Price column, "[Price] – [Discount] > 0" is not. (Use List/Item Validation instead. See Chapter 9.)
- A new or edited validation formula will not report errors for existing items. Validation only occurs when an item is added or edited.

Column Validations Cannot be Applied to All Column Types

Column Validations can only be added to columns types that define a single piece of data, such as a number, date or text.

Column Validations can be added to:

- Single line of text

- Choice (but not with "Checkboxes (allow multiple selections)")
- Number
- Currency
- Date and Time

Column Validations cannot be added to:

- Multiple lines of text
- Choice columns that using "Checkboxes (allow multiple selections)"
- Lookup
- Yes/No (check box)
- Person or Group
- Hyperlink or Picture
- Calculated (calculation based on other columns)
- Task Outcome
- External Data
- Managed Metadata

Column Validation Without Formulas

Before writing formulas, check to see if SharePoint has a built-in feature to do the needed validation. Validating a numeric column to be greater than or equal to zero is easy. Just set the "Min" value to 0.

Must be Greater Than Zero

You can specify a minimum and maximum allowed value:

Min: 0   Max:

What if the value in column must be more than 0? If you know the smallest acceptable value is 1, enter 1, otherwise enter a really small number. ☺

You can specify a minimum and maximum allowed value:

Min: .00000000001   Max:

Limiting Data to a Limited Set of Values

SharePoint offers several column types to limit a user's entry to a predefined listed of values. A Choice column has the list of values that is stored with the column. A Lookup column has the list of values stored in another list in the same site. A Managed Metadata column has a list of values stored in a central location available to all of your SharePoint sites.

Built-in "Select from a list" columns:

The type of information in this column is:
- ◉ Single line of text
- ○ Multiple lines of text
- ○ Choice (menu to choose from)
- ○ Number (1, 1.0, 100)
- ○ Currency ($, ¥, €)
- ○ Date and Time
- ○ Lookup (information already on this site)
- ○ Yes/No (check box)
- ○ Person or Group
- ○ Hyperlink or Picture
- ○ Calculated (calculation based on other columns)
- ○ Task Outcome
- ○ External Data
- ○ Managed Metadata

In addition to those three column types, the Person or Group column type lets you limit a user's select to "real people" in your Active Directory or to a group of users in a single AD or SharePoint group.

If none of these options work for your project, then you can write a validation formula that can range from something similar to a Choice list to a formula with very complex logic.

General Validation Formula Rules

There are always a few rules and exceptions...

- A validation formula must return True or False. The formula can be an IF function that returns True or False:

    =IF([Price] > 5, true, false)

    or as simple as a Boolean comparison (they are always either True or False):

    =[Price] > 5

- Column validations can only be added to Single Line of Text, Number, Choice (Drop-Down menu or Radio buttons, but not Checkboxes), Currency and Date and Time columns.
- Expressions are generally Excel compatible, but not all Excel functions can be used.
- Field names without special symbols can be typed as is or typed in square brackets.

    = Price * [Qty] > 100

- Field names with spaces or symbols must be enclosed in square brackets.
  =OR([Sales Region] = 1, [Sales Region] = 2)
  = [Retail Price] * [Order Qty] > 100
- Text comparisons are not case sensitive.
  =OR(status = "a", status="c")   is true for either "A" or "a" or "C" or "c".
  - o If you need case sensitive comparisons, use the EXACT() function or see a workaround in the "Calculation Validation Examples" chapter.
- In a column validation, the formula cannot refer to another column.
- In a list / library validation the formula can refer to other columns in the same item.

Guidelines and Tips for Validation Formulas

Validation formulas ask questions that are either true or false. These can be simple comparisons or involve complex logic.

Some things are always True or False, or at least fairly obvious:

- =True
  - o Not much of a validation! All entries are accepted!
- = FirstName = "Mike"
  - o Only true if "Mike" was entered in the "FirstName" column. (SharePoint text comparisons are not case sensitive. This formula would also be true for "mike" and "MIKE".
  - o For case sensitive comparisons use the EXACT() function.
    =EXACT(FirstName, "Mike")
- = (FirstName = "Mike")
  - o Same as above, but makes clear the use of the equal signs.
- = Price > 5
  - o Operators like ">", "<" and "=" return a True or False result.

Examples of more complex formulas using the AND, OR and NOT Boolean operators:

= AND (Price > 5, Price < 10)

= OR (State = "OH", State = "NY")

= NOT(OR (State = "OH", State = "NY"))   (Any state except for "OH" and "NY".)

Incorrect validation formulas:

- =5

- o This does not return True or False. The formula returns a number, not a True or False. Non-zero numbers are always treated as True. Zero is always treated as False. (See the first "Tricky" validation below for an interesting use of returning a number in a validation formula.)
- = "abc"
  - o As "abc" cannot be converted into a True, False, zero or non-zero number, it is treated as "False". This column will never pass validation!
    A correct version might be: = Name="abc"

Tricky validation formulas:

- = Qty − 7
  - o In the "Incorrect validation formulas" list above we saw that a zero is treated as a False and a non-zero is treated as a True. For this example, if the "Qty" column contains a 7, then an error is displayed. "7-7" returns zero, which is treated as "False".

    Qty   [7   ]

    Column Validation Failed.
- = IF(Qty < 0, True, False)
  - o Not really tricky, but may add some clarity for the next person trying to figure it out. This is the same as "= Qty < 0".

Notes:

- A new or edited validation formula will not report errors for existing items. Validation only occurs when an item is added or edited.

7.   Column Validation Examples

The real core of this book are the examples. In this chapter we have more than 30 examples of Column Validation formulas.

Examples in this chapter:

- Limit time for user updates.
- Boolean operations
    - Examples Using "OR"
    - Examples Using "AND"
    - Examples Using "AND" and "OR"
    - Examples Using "NOT"
- Testing for Empty Columns
    - Yes/No
    - Dates
    - ISBLANK()
- Working with Dates
    - Date Must be in the Future
    - Date Must be in the Future "x" Days
    - Date Must be in the Future "x" Days and not on a Weekend
    - Test Against a Specified Date
    - Date Must be Between Now and the End of the Current Year
    - Date Must be Within the Next 30 days
    - Date Must be the Last Day of the Month
    - Date Must be the First Day of the Month
    - Date Must be the Third Tuesday of the Month
    - Date Can Only be a Weekday
    - Date Can Only be Monday or Wednesday

- o   Entered Date Must be for this Year
- o   Date Must be Current Or Next Month Only
- Working with Numbers
  - o   Testing for Numbers in Custom Increments
  - o   Limit the Number of Decimal Places Entered
- Working with Text
  - o   Testing for Text Length
  - o   Testing for a Valid State/Province (or other code)
  - o   Test to Require an Uppercase or Lowercase Letter
- Examples Using Pattern Matching
  - o   Must start with an "a" or "A" and the third character must be a "c" or "C"
  - o   Match a Phone Number Pattern of xxx-xxx-xxxx
  - o   Match a Phone Number Pattern of xxx-xxx-xxxx and Limit the Length
  - o   Match a Phone Number and Make Sure Only Digits Have Been Used

Limit the Time for Updates

If you have a list where the data is very time sensitive, you may want to limit updates to only the next "x hours" or "y days" after the item was created. To add this edit restriction, the validation formula for the Created column only needs to compare the Created date and time to a calculated limit.

Here's the validation formula that lets the user make changes for up to 12 hours after creating the list item.

```
=Created + .5 <= NOW()
```

What if you, the Site Owner, wanted to make changes after 12 hours? You would need to delete the validation formula, make the edit, and then put the formula back.

A couple of things to consider when working with dates and times:

- TODAY() and NOW() are current times, and are reevaluated only on each item edit.
- TODAY() is the date and time as of midnight. Assuming today is 4/19/2018 the TODAY () function would return 4/19/2018 12:00 AM.
- The Created column is a date and a time column, not just a date.
- When doing date math, 1 is 24 hours, and .5 is 12 hours.
- If you are displaying your Created column as "Date" and not "Date and Time", remember these are just formatting options. The full date and time is still being stored in Created.

Boolean Functions

While you can use the Excel-like AND, OR and NOT functions in Column Validation formulas, they can only refer to the current column. For example, in the Total column you can test that the [Total] must be greater than 0, but you cannot test to see if [Total] is greater than zero AND the [Total] is greater than the [Discount].

Examples Using "OR"

The OR function accepts two or more Boolean tests that each return True or False. The OR function returns True if any one of the tests is True.

=OR(YourFieldName="A", YourFieldName="C", YourFieldName="E")

=OR(State="OH", State="IN", State="KY", State="MI")

=OR(Qty=5, Qty=10, Qty=20)

If you have a long list of conditions to test, such as all fifty states, then take a look at the "Testing for a Valid State (or other code)" example later in this chapter.

Examples Using "AND"

The AND function accepts two or more Boolean tests that each return True or False. AND returns True if all of the tests are True.

=AND(YourFieldName > "A", YourFieldName < "M")

YourFieldName value must be between "A" and "M", but not include "A" or "M".

=AND(Qty > 5, Qty < 100, Qty <> 47)

Qty must be between 5 and 100, but not 47.

Examples Using "AND" and "OR"

The AND and OR functions can be nested to build more complex tests.

If the acceptable status codes are A through M, R and Z then you could test with this:

124

```
=OR( AND( StatusCode >= "A", StatusCode <= "M" ),

      StatusCode = "R",

      StatusCode = "Z"

    )
```

Note: SharePoint formulas are generally not case sensitive. The letter "a" is a valid status code in the above formula.

An alternate to the OR/AND example:

There's always more than one solution! You could use a string of status codes and the FIND or SEARCH functions. As the FIND and SEARCH functions return an error if the value is not found, you will need to wrap them in a ISERROR function. (FIND is case sensitive while SEARCH is not.)

```
=NOT( ISERROR( SEARCH( StatusCode, "ABCDEFGHIJKLMRZ" ) ) )
```

If the StatusCode column is not set to be Required, you will need to add an ISBLANK or LEN test to the above.

```
=AND( NOT( ISBLANK( StatusCode ) ),
       NOT( ISERROR( SEARCH( StatusCode, "ABCDEFGHIJKLMRZ" ) )
       )
```

Or:

```
=AND( LEN( StatusCode ) > 0,
       NOT( ISERROR( SEARCH( StatusCode, "ABCDEFGHIJKLMRZ" ) )
       )
```

Examples Using "NOT"

The NOT function negates, or reverses, the Boolean value it contains.

If we have locations in every state except for "HI" and "AK" then use either of the following.

```
=OR( [State]="AL", [State]="AZ",[State]="AR",[State]="CA", … with all 48 states with locations…
```

Or using ANDs with "not equal to":

```
=AND( [State] <> "HI", [State] <> "AK" )
```

Or using NOT:

```
=NOT( OR( [State]="HI", [State]="AK" ) )
```

Testing for Empty Columns

ISBLANK() will test for columns with no entered data. The ISBLANK function, like all other SharePoint functions, only works on a column that can be seen by Calculated Columns.

ISBLANK()

The ISBLANK function returns true if the column is blank.

    =ISBLANK([SomeData])

To test to see if there is data:

    =NOT(ISBLANK([SomeData])

Tip! In most cases, the following are equivalent to ISBLANK([SomeData]):

    LEN([SomeData]) = 0

    [SomeData] = ""

The following are unsupported column types in SharePoint formulas, and therefore cannot be tested with ISBLANK():

- Lookup columns.
- Multivalued columns. For example: Choice columns with the "checkboxes" option enabled.
- Multiple lines of text columns.
- Person or Group columns. (These have two values: display name and user ID.)
- Hyperlink columns. (These have two values: display text, and the URL.)
- Managed Metadata columns.
- Hidden columns. Internal columns used by SharePoint.

Yes/No Columns?

While Yes/No columns are supported by Calculated Columns, they always have a default value, and are never blank.

Dates?

Blank date columns will be treated as 12/31/1899 in all date calculations.

When the column [SomeDate] is empty:

- TEXT([SomeDate],"dddd") returns "Saturday", not an error.

        o   Rewrite as: IF(ISBLANK([SomeDate]) , "", TEXT([SomeDate],"dddd"))
- [SomeDate] + 30 returns "1/30/1900".
        o   Rewrite as: IF(ISBLANK([SomeDate]) , "", [SomeDate] + 30)

Working with Dates

Before writing validation formulas that use dates, read the following sections in the "Tips for Formulas" chapter:

- "Converting a Date and Time to a Date"
- "Dealing with Blank Dates"

Date Must be in the Future

If your users are just entering Month, Day and Year, then the following will work.

   =[YourFieldName] > TODAY()   I.e. Today = 1/15/2018

If they are entering dates and times, then you will need to test against the NOW() function. NOW returns the current date and time.

   =[YourFieldName] > NOW()   I.e Now = 1/15/2018 4:12 PM

Date Must be in the Future "x" Days

This is the same as the above with just a little math. If the entered date must be at least three days in the future just add the number of days as a whole number or a decimal.

   =[YourFieldName] >TODAY() + 3

   =[YourFieldName] >TODAY() + 3.5   (3 days and 12 hours)

Date Must be in the Future "x" Days and not on a Weekend

This is the same as the above formula with a second test to see if the date is a weekend day. (When using WEEKDAY with option "2", Saturday is a 6 and Sunday is a 7.)

In this example a user can request a day off as long as it is at least three days in the future and not a weekend day. (They get the weekends off anyway, right?)

=AND([Requested Day Off] >TODAY() + 3, WEEKDAY([Requested Day Off], 2) < 6)

Test Against a Specified Date

Sometimes you have absolute dates…

=[YourFieldName] > DATEVALUE("1/1/2020")

Or

=[YourFieldName] > DATE(2020,1,1)

Date Must be Between Now and the End of the Current Year

By using the DATEVALUE or DATE functions you can create a yearend date from today's date.

=[YourFieldName] <= DATEVALUE("12/31/" & YEAR(TODAY()))

Or

=[YourFieldName] <= DATE(YEAR(TODAY()), 12, 31)

Note that this creates a date with a time of midnight. I.e. 12/31/2018 12:00 AM. If the YourFiledName column is storing both date and time, then use a test like this one:

=[YourFieldName] < DATE(YEAR(TODAY()), 12, 31) + 1

This tests to see if the YourFieldName date is less than 1/1/2019 12:00 AM.

Date Must be Within the Next 30 days

If entered dates must be between today's date and X number of dates in the future, you will need two tests inside of an AND function.

=AND([YourFieldName] >= TODAY(), [YourFieldName] <= TODAY() + 30)

See the note in the previous example for working with date and time.

Date Must be the Last Day of the Month

There are two "tricks" in this little example:

- The DATE function treats setting the "day" value to "0" as a date one less than the first of the month.
- We can step backwards one day from the next month by also adding one to the current month.

=[yourDateColumn] = DATE(YEAR([yourDateColumn]), MONTH([yourDateColumn])+1, 0)

Or if your column includes both date and time:

=INT([yourDateColumn]) = DATE(YEAR([yourDateColumn]), MONTH([yourDateColumn])+1, 0)

No IFs are needed as the equality equal sign in the middle of the formula will generate a True or False response. (Things are equal, or they are not.)

Date Must be the First Day of the Month

This one is too easy! The DAY function returns the day of the month as a number.

=DAY([yourDateColumn]) = 1

Date Must be the Third Tuesday of the Month

Let's start with an example that tests for the first Tuesday of the month. Assuming a column named "TheDate":

```
=TheDate = DATE( YEAR(TheDate), MONTH(TheDate), 1 ) +
          IF( WEEKDAY( DATE( YEAR(TheDate), MONTH(TheDate), 1 ) ) <= 3 ,
              3,
              3+7)
          - WEEKDAY( DATE( YEAR(TheDate), MONTH(TheDate), 1 ) )
```

Notes:

- The default numbering for WEEKDAY is: Sunday = 1, Monday = 2, Tuesday = 3, etc. Change the "3" in the above formula to your choice of day numbers.
- The formula starts by getting the first day of the entered month (DATE(YEAR(TheDate),MONTH(TheDate),1)) and adds the offset to the first Tuesday.

- The IF tests to see if the first week contains a Tuesday (3) and if does not, it adds seven to get the Tuesday of the next week. It starts from the first of the month:
  DATE(YEAR(TheDate),MONTH(TheDate),1)
- If TheDate equals our calculated date, then the user entered a first Tuesday of the month.

◻ Column Validation

Specify the formula that you want to use to validate the data in this column when new items are saved to this list. The formula must evaluate to TRUE for validation to pass.

Example: If your column is called "Company Name" a valid formula would be [Company Name]="My Company".

Learn more about proper syntax for formulas.

Formula:

```
=TheDate = Date( Year(TheDate),
Month(TheDate), 1 ) +
             IF( WEEKDAY( Date(
Year(TheDate), Month(TheDate), 1 ) ) <= 3 ,
             3,
             3+7)
             - WEEKDAY( Date(
Year(TheDate), Month(TheDate), 1 ) )
```

Type descriptive text that explains what is needed for this column's value to be considered valid.

User message:

Must be the first Tuesday of the month!

For the Nth Tuesday

For the Nth Tuesday add a multiple of 7 to the first Tuesday. For the second Tuesday add "7" days to the first Tuesday. For the third Tuesday add "2 * 7" days to the first Tuesday.

```
=TheDate = Date( Year(TheDate), Month(TheDate), 1 ) +
        IF( WEEKDAY( Date( Year(TheDate), Month(TheDate), 1 ) ) <= 3 ,
           3,
           3+7)
        - WEEKDAY( Date( Year(TheDate), Month(TheDate), 1 ) )
        + ( 2 * 7 )
```

Date Can Only be a Weekday

There are several ways to solve this using the WEEKDAY function.

You can test to see if the day is a Saturday or a Sunday:

```
=NOT( OR( WEEKDAY( [yourDateColumn], 2 )=6, WEEKDAY([yourDateColumn],2)=7 ) )
```

You can test to the see if day is less than a Saturday:

```
=WEEKDAY( [yourDateColumn], 2 ) < 6
```

Note: The second parameter of the WEEKDAY function controls how days are numbered. Here's the list of values as seen in Excel:

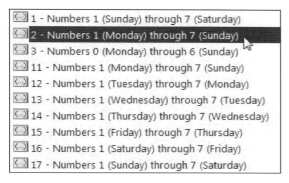

Date Can Only be Monday or Wednesday

Just need to add an OR to test for both days. With the second parameter of WEEKDAY set to 2, Mondays are a 1.

> = OR(WEEKDAY([yourDateColumn], 2) = 1, WEEKDAY([yourDateColumn], 2) = 3))

Entered Date Must be for this Year

As an example, we have a column named SomeDate that when entered must be for the current year. In this example, the current year is 2018 and the user entered a 2019 date:

The formula to validate our "current year" requirement would look like this:

> =YEAR(SomeDate) = YEAR(TODAY())

Here is the column's page with the formula and the "user message":

⊟ Column Validation

Specify the formula that you want to use to validate the data in this column when new items are saved to this list. The formula must evaluate to TRUE for validation to pass.

Example: If your column is called "Company Name" a valid formula would be [Company Name]="My Company".

Learn more about proper syntax for formulas.

Formula:

```
=YEAR(SomeDate)=YEAR(TODAY())
```

Type descriptive text that explains what is needed for this column's value to be considered valid.

User message:

```
Date must be for the current year.
```

Date Must be Current Or Next Month Only

This example tests to see if an entered date is between the first of this month and the end of next month.

```
=AND( [MyColumnName] >= DATE( YEAR(TODAY() ), MONTH(TODAY()), 1 ),
      [MyColumnName] <   DATE( YEAR(TODAY() ), MONTH(TODAY()) + 2, 1 ) )
```

The first item in the AND tests the date against the current year, current month, and the 1st day. The second item tests the date against the current year, two months in the future, and the 1st day of that month.

I.e., if today is 4/12/2018, this would look like this:

```
AND( mycolmun >= 4/1/2018, mycolumn < 6/1/2018 )
```

Working with Numbers

Here are a few examples of testing for number patterns.

- Testing for Numbers in Custom Increments
- Limit the Number of Decimal Places Entered
- Single Line of Text Value Must be Numeric
- Part of a String Must be Numeric

Also see the math, trigonometry, financial and statistical functions covered in "Tips for Formulas" chapter.

Testing for Numbers for Custom Increments

How do you test for numbers that can only be steps of 5 (5, 10, 15, …) or steps of 30 (30, 60, 90, …) or even steps of .25 (.25, .50, .75, …)? There is the ROUND function, but it only rounds off to the nearest decimal place:

    =ROUND(33.33, 0)   returns 33

    =ROUND(55.55, 0)   returns 56

    =ROUND(55.55, 1)   returns 55.6   (The nearest one decimal place.)

If you know a trick, you can round off to the nearest 10, 100 or 1000. Just use a negative number of decimal places!

    =ROUND(55.55, -1)   returns 60

    =ROUND(54, -1)   returns 50

    =ROUND(555555, -2)   returns 55600   (Rounds to the nearest 100)

To round to any other number other than 10, we just need to divide, round and then multiply. For example, to get the nearest multiple of 30:

    =ROUND(100 / 30, 0) * 30   returns 90

    =ROUND(110 / 30, 0) * 30   returns 120

When you just want to round to a whole number, you can also use the INT function. Notice there is no digits parameter.

    =INT(110 / 30) * 30   returns 120

To Validate numbers to be a multiple of "X"

A validation formula must return True or False, not a number, so just test the rounded value to the value in the column. For this example, assume we are validating a column named "Delivery Days" that must be 0, 30, 60, etc.

    =ROUND([Delivery Days] / 30, 0) * 30 = [Delivery Days]
        returns True for 30 and 60 and False for 45.

Or

    =INT([Delivery Days] / 30) * 30 = [Delivery Days]
        returns True for 30 and 60 and False for 45.

Limit the Number of Decimal Places Entered

While SharePoint number columns can be formatted to display only "x" decimal places, the user can still enter more digits, and SharePoint will still store all of the digits.

In this example the user typed "1234.56789" into a column that was formatted to show two decimal places. Notice that the Calculated Column next to it still sees the value typed by the user. The "Number of decimal places" option only formats the number, it does not truncate it or round it.

A validation formula to test the number of decimal places.

There are two formulas that can validate that no more than "x" decimal places have been entered by the user. The first uses ROUND and the number of decimal places while the second uses INT and a multiplier. Use 10 for 1 decimal place, 100 for 2 decimal places, 1000 for 3 decimal places, etc.

=ROUND(Price, 2) = Price

=INT(Price * 100) / 100 = Price

Price   [1234.5678]

Do not enter more than two decimal places.

This same validation can be used to make sure the user typed in even 10s, 100s or 1000s. For the ROUND version just use a negative number of decimal places and for the INT version just reverse the order of the multiply and divide.

=ROUND(Price, -2) = Price

=INT(Price / 100) * 100 = Price

Price   [123]

Must be an even multiple of 100!

The INT version of the above example can even be used to test fractional amounts. For example, if wanted to allow values to the nearest 1/4th, edit the formula to divide by four and multiply by four.

=INT(Price / 4) * 4 = Price

The following values are valid: .25, 1.25, 3.5, 10, 12.75

The following values are not valid: .1, 1.1, 4.9, 2.333

Single Line of Text Value Must be Numeric

If you have a column that can be either text (maybe "na" or "none") or a number, you will need a test to limit entries to just those values. The ISNUMBER function only works on numeric columns, which makes it sound a bit useless. For Single Line of Text columns you will need to convert the text value to a number by adding it to zero, or by using the VALUE function.

=OR(SomeTextColumn = "na", ISNUMBER(**0 +** SomeTextColumn))

=OR(SomeTextColumn = "na", ISNUMBER(**VALUE**(SomeTextColumn)))

If blanks are not allowed, either set the column to be a Required column or add an ISBLANK test.

=AND(NOT(ISBLANK(SomeTextColumn)),

　　　OR(SomeTextColumn = "na", ISNUMBER(0 + SomeTextColumn))

　　　)

Part of a String Must be Numeric

If the 4th to 6th characters of a part number must be numeric, pull out those characters using the MID function and then test the numeric part as in the previous example.

=ISNUMBER(0 + MID(StatusCode, 4, 3))

Notes:

- The MID function returns 3 characters starting at the 4th character.
- Zero is added to the result to convert the 3 characters to a numeric value.
- ISNUMBER then tests to see if the result is a number (or an error).
- This does not test for length of the numeric section. "aa-123" is valid for this formula. "aa-21a" is not. The following values would all pass this validation:
    aa-12, aa-12345, aa-123-bb, aa-123cde
    These values do not:
    aa-a, 123, aa-12a123

For a more complex version of this pattern, see the phone number validation examples later in this chapter.

Working with Text

The examples that follow show the use of these text related functions:

- LEN

- FIND and SEARCH
- UPPER
- CODE and ASCII
- CONCATENATE and "&"

Testing for Text Length

While a SharePoint column can limit the maximum number of characters entered, it cannot test for multiple length options or prevent shorter values from being entered.

As an example, if your part numbers are always 9 characters long:

=LEN(YourFieldName) = 9

If the part numbers can be 9 or 12 characters long:

=OR(LEN(YourFieldName) = 9, LEN(YourFieldName) = 12)

Testing for a Valid State/Province (or other code)

Writing nested Ifs or complex ORs can often be simplified with a "trick" or two. Without a trick, testing for a valid state code would require a long formula:

=OR([State]="AL", [State]="AK",[State]="AZ",[State]="AR",[State]="CA", …

Trivia question… how many two letter postal codes are there?

If we store the list of states as a single string of states separated by commas, we can use the FIND command to find the numeric position of the state and if it is greater than zero, the code is valid. Maybe something like this:

=FIND([State], "AL,AK,AZ,AR,CA …more states here!... ,WV,WI") > 0

The FIND function is not real friendly... if there is not a match it returns an error. To deal with this we will add an IFERROR that returns a zero if FIND returns an error.

```
=IFERROR(
   FIND( [State], "AL,AK,AZ,AR,CA, ...more states here!... ,WV,WI"
   )
  ,0)  > 0
```

There is also another little problem in that if a user just entered "A" or "C", that would also be considered a match. To solve this problem, we will add a comma to our search pattern so we are searching for "AL," or "CA,". Now we can find our exact match. Note the extra comma after "WI". Each state code will need a pattern of two letters and a comma for this to work.

```
=IFERROR(
   FIND( [State] & "," , "AL,AK,AZ,AR,CA, ...more states here!... ,WV,WI,"
   )
  ,0)  > 0
```

If you have really creative users, they could enter "AR,CA" and have a match. To prevent this, we can add an "AND" to test the length of their state code.

```
=AND( LEN( [State] ) = 2,
      IFERROR(
       FIND( [State] & "," , "AL,AK,AZ,AR,CA, ...more states here!... ,WV,WI," )
      ,0)  > 0
      )
```

So, finally, here's the complete solution:

```
=AND( LEN( [State] ) = 2,
      IFERROR(
    FIND( [State] & "," , "AL,AK,AZ,AR,CA,CO,CT,DE,FL,GA,HI,ID,IL,IN,IA,KS,KY, LA,
                   ME,MD,MA,MI,MN,MS,MO,MT,NE,NV,NH,NJ,NM,NY, NC,ND,
                   OH,OK,OR,PA,RI,SC,SD,TN,TX,UT,VT,VA,WA,WV,WI,")
      ,0)  > 0
      )
```

Note: FIND is case sensitive! The validation above would fail if the user entered lowercase letters. If you wanted to allow both upper and lower case entries, replace [State] with UPPER([STATE]).

Formula:

```
=AND(LEN(State)=2,IFERROR(FIND(State&",","
AL,AK,AZ,AR,CA,CO,CT,DE,FL,GA,HI,ID,IL,IN,IA,KS
,KY,LA,ME,MD,MA,MI,MN,MS,MO,MT,NE,NV,NH,
NJ,NM,NY,NC,ND,OH,OK,OR,PA,RI,SC,SD,TN,TX,
UT,VT,VA,WA,WV,WI,"),0)>0)
```

User message:

Not a valid State

Title *   Test

State   KE

Not a valid State

Test to Require an Uppercase or Lowercase Letter

SharePoint formulas are generally case insensitive and treat an "A" as equal to an "a". While the formula below looks like it would limit an entry to be an uppercase letter, it returns True for both upper and lowercase letters.

=AND([SomeLetterColumn] >= "A", [SomeLetterColumn] <= "Z")

To work around this case insensitive "feature", we need to covert the letter in the column to the number that represents the letter. Using the CODE function, an "A" is a 65 and a "Z" is a 90.

=AND(CODE([SomeLetterColumn]) >= 65, CODE([SomeLetterColumn]) <= 90)

Notes:

- The CODE function only checks the first letter. Both "A" and "Abc" would be accepted.
- To find the numeric value of a letter, such as "b", open Excel and in a cell type =CODE("b")
- The numeric values are from the ASCII encoding of text.
- To find the letter or symbol that belongs to a number use =ASCII(65)

Examples Using Pattern Matching

There are two handy functions, SEARCH and FIND, that can be used to check to see if text matches a pattern. Examples of pattern matching include phone numbers, ZIP codes and part numbers. These often have more than one acceptable pattern and a simple length test is probably not enough to validate these values.

The SEARCH function:

- If there is a match, the function returns the position of the match as an integer. If every character is to be matched, you would typically test for "=1". For matching within the text then test for ">0".

- If there is no match, the function returns ERROR, therefore it must be wrapped inside of an ISERROR function. As we will have a match if there is no error, the ISERROR must be wrapped inside of a NOT function.
- Matches a pattern using the "*" and "?" characters. The "*" matches zero more characters and the "?" matches exactly one character.
- To match an asterisk or question mark character, prefix the symbols with "~".
    - Example: "a~?b?c" matches "a?bxc" but not "axbxc".
- An "*" is assumed to be appended to the end of the match pattern. To limit the length use the AND and the LEN functions.
    - Example: =AND(LEN(partnumber)=5, SEARCH("a~?b?c", partnumber)=1)
    - As SEARCH returns an error if there is no match we need to deal with the error:
      =AND(LEN(partnumber)=5,**NOT(ISERROR(**SEARCH("a?b?c",partnumber)=1)))
- The comparison is not case sensitive.
- Documentation for SEARCH: https://support.office.com/en-us/article/SEARCH-SEARCHB-functions-9ab04538-0e55-4719-a72e-b6f54513b495 (or just search for "EXCEL SEARCH")
- The third parameter is optional and specifies where in the text to start the search.
    - To see if there is a "B" somewhere starting with the 6th character:
      =SEARCH("B",partnumber, 6)

The FIND Function:

- The FIND function is similar to the SEARCH function with two differences;
    - FIND is case sensitive.
    - FIND does not support wild cards.
- Documentation for FIND: https://support.office.com/en-us/article/FIND-FINDB-functions-c7912941-af2a-4bdf-a553-d0d89b0a0628 (or just search for "EXCEL FIND")

Note: While it would be very handy, neither Excel or SharePoint have a Regular Expression pattern match function.

Must start with an "a" or "A" and the third character must be a "c" or "C"

=NOT(ISERROR(SEARCH("A?C", YourFieldName) = 1))

Matches: abc AbC aXc a6c aBcDEF

Does not match: bbb abb ac a

Note: Use the FIND function if you need case sensitive matches.

Match a Phone Number Pattern of xxx-xxx-xxxx

Although SharePoint functions do not support Regular Expressions, the SEARCH function does support pattern matching using wild card symbols. (See more on SEARCH in the "Examples Using Pattern Matching" topic earlier in this chapter.)

If you need to match a USA style phone number, and letters or digits are acceptable, this formula will do what you need:

```
=NOT( ISERROR( SEARCH("???-???-????", YourFieldName) = 1 ))
```

Matches: 123-123-1234   aaa-aaa-aaaa   123-123-12344444   abc123-123-1234def

Does not match: 1231231234   123-123-123   123

Note: The user could type letters or digits, or type extra characters, and this would still be a match. Keep reading for a better, and more complex, solutions.

Match a Phone Number Pattern of xxx-xxx-xxxx and Limit the Length

This formula adds a length check to make sure the phone number is exactly 12 characters long.

```
=AND( NOT( ISERROR( SEARCH("???-???-????", YourFieldName) = 1 )),
       LEN(YourFieldName) = 12 )
```

Matches: 123-123-1234   123-abc-1234

Does not match: 123-123-12345   123   1231231234   abc123-123-1234def

Match a Phone Number and Make Sure Only Digits Have Been Used

The examples above match for patterns of characters, any characters. If we really want the user to only enter phone numbers using digits, then we have a bit more work to do.

The first example here is not a true pattern match. It just extracts the characters we think should be digits and tries to multiply them by any number. If that fails (the ISERROR test), then one or more of the characters is not a number.

```
=NOT( ISERROR( 1 * CONCATENATE( MID( YourFieldName, 1, 3),
                                MID( YourFieldName, 5, 3),
                                MID( YourFieldName, 9, 4 ) ) ) )
```

Matches: 123-123-1234   123x123x1234   123-123-1234xxxxx

Does not match: abc-123-1234

- The value being tested should match the pattern of 111-111-1111
- Each of the MIDs pulls out each numeric part of the phone number as text.
- The CONCATENATE combines the three pieces of text. (I.e. 1111111111)
- The "1 *" performs a math operation against the full number, if that fails then there is a non-number in the string.
- There is one weakness, the user could type a dot, and we would still find a valid number. (111-1.1-1111) If you want to prevent this, after the third MID add another item to the concatenation that includes a decimal point and a digit. (".5"). If the user types a decimal point, there will now be two decimal points in the number, and that will be an error.

The next example combines the earlier pattern and a length match with a numeric test. The addition of the SEARCH function insures that the separators are dashes.

```
=AND( NOT( ISERROR( SEARCH( "???-???-????", YourFieldName ) = 1) ),
      LEN( YourFieldName ) = 12,
      NOT( ISERROR( 1 * CONCATENATE( MID( YourFieldName, 1, 3),
                                     MID( YourFieldName, 5, 3),
                                     MID( YourFieldName, 9, 4) ) ) ) )
```

There are all kinds of variations of these formulas. To match this phone number pattern, "(123) 123-1234", we will need to change the SEARCH, the length and the position numbers of each section.

```
=AND( NOT( ISERROR( SEARCH( "(???) ???-????", YourFieldName ) = 1) ),
      LEN( YourFieldName ) = 14,
      NOT( ISERROR( 1 * CONCATENATE( MID( YourFieldName, 2, 3),
                                     MID( YourFieldName, 7, 3),
                                     MID( YourFieldName, 11, 4) ) ) ) )
```

8.   List/Library Item Validation

Column Validation formulas can only reference the current column's value. They cannot test the current column against other columns. Item validation formulas can access any Calculated Column compatible column in a single item in a list or library. These formulas cannot access other rows in the same list.

List/Library Item Validation Limitations

- Item Validation formulas have a maximum length of 1024 characters in all versions.
- A new or edited Validation formula will not report errors for existing items. Validation only occurs when an item is added or edited.
- Item Validation formulas can only reference these column types: (Same list as Calculated Columns. See the "Workflow Workarounds" chapter for ways to access other column types.)
    - Single line of text
    - Choice (but not with "Checkboxes (allow multiple selections)")
    - Number
    - Currency
    - Date and Time

An Example of an Item Validation

For a Task list you might want these restrictions:

- Due Date must be after Start Date.
- Start Date must be on or after Created date.

The formula might look like this:

   =AND([Due Date] > [Start Date], [Start Date] >= Created)

The error message might look like this:

   Check your dates! Start must be before Due and Start must be on or after Created.

The validation would look like this:

The user would see this after entering invalid dates and clicking Save.

Task Name *	Do some work!
Start Date	2/15/2018
Due Date	1/30/2018
Assigned To	Enter names or email addresses...

SHOW MORE

Save   Cancel

Check your dates! Start must be before Due and Start must be on or after Created

To set List/Library Item validations

Classic UI: Click the Library Ribbon, LIST/LIBRARY, List/Library Settings and then Validation Settings.

Modern UI: Click the Settings (Gear) menu and Library Settings.

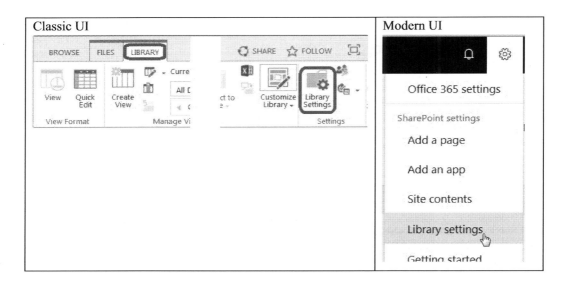

Both the Classic UI and the Modern UI will then take you to the list or library settings page where you can define a "master" validation formula that controls if a list/library item can be saved..

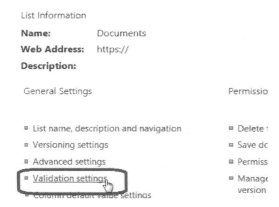

9.   List/Library Item Validation Examples

Every example from the "Column Validation Examples" chapter can be used in List/Library Item Validation formulas. While Column Validation formulas can only see their one column's data, List/Library Item Validation formulas can see all columns in the current item that are accessible from a Calculated Column.

Boolean Functions

Unlike Column Validation where you can only refer to the current column. Item Validation formulas can access other columns in the same item. For example, you can validate that the [Tax] column must be greater than zero when the [State] column equals Ohio.

Examples Using "OR"

The OR function accepts two or more Boolean tests that each return True or False. The OR function returns True if any one of the tests is True. If the result is True, the user can save the list item.

    =OR(State = "OH", TaxAmount > 0)

    =OR([Total Due] > 0, [Credit Balance] > 0)

Examples Using "AND"

The AND function accepts two or more Boolean tests that each return True or False. AND returns True if all of the tests are True. In the following examples, both of the AND conditions must evaluate to True or the list item cannot be saved.

=AND([Ship Date] < Now(), [Order Status] = "Shipped")

=AND(Qty>0, [Item Status] = "Active")

Examples Using "AND" and "OR"

AND and OR functions can be nested to build more complex tests.

If the acceptable status codes are A through M or State equals Ohio, then you can save the list item.

=OR(AND(StatusCode >= "A", StatusCode <= "M"),

     State = "OHIO"

)

Note: SharePoint formulas are not case sensitive. The letter "a" is a valid status code in the above formula.

Examples Using "NOT"

The NOT function negates, or reverses, the Boolean value it contains.

Example: If the Status cannot equal "Inactive" and State cannot equal "OH", then the user cannot save the list item.

Using ANDs with "not equal to":

=AND([Status] <> "Inactive", [State] <> "OH")

Or using NOT:

=NOT(OR([Status]="Inactive", [State]="OH"))

Testing for Empty Columns

If Field A has a Value then Field B must have a Value

In this example, if the City column has a value, then the State column must also have a value.

> =IF(NOT(ISBLANK(City)), IF(ISBLANK(State), FALSE, TRUE), TRUE)

Or

> =NOT(AND(NOT(ISBLANK(City)), ISBLANK(State)))

Both of the above return True (user can save the item) if City is blank or City and State are both populated. If City is populated, but State is not, then this returns False and the item cannot be saved.

Working with Dates

A common list item Validation is the comparison of date columns to make sure the make sense. The ShipDate must be before the DeliverDate and both must be after the OrderDate.

Test If One Date is Greater than Another

End Dates should never be earlier than Start Dates… but users can be pretty creative with date entries. Basic date comparisons are pretty simple.

> =[End Date] > [Start Date]

The above is either True or False, so it is a suitable validation… but only if both dates will always be entered.

| Start Date | 3/5/2017 |
| End Date | 1/20/2017 |

Save   Cancel

Cannot finish before we have started!

What if the End Date has not been entered yet?

Start Date   [3/5/2017   ] 🔲

End Date   [   ] 🔲

                              [Save]   [Cancel]

Cannot finish before we have started!

We will even get the same error if neither date has been entered! We may actually have three requirements for validation, depending on your requirements.

1. Both Start Date and End Date must be blank, or…
2. The End Date must be blank, but not the start date, or…
3. Both dates must exist and the End Date cannot be before the Start Date.

Here is an Item Validation formula to enforce these requirements:

=OR(
     AND(ISBLANK(StartDate), ISBLANK(EndDate)),
     AND(NOT(ISBLANK(StartDate)), ISBLANK(EndDate)),
     AND(NOT(ISBLANK(StartDate)), NOT(ISBLANK(EndDate)), EndDate > StartDate)
)

We use the OR because any one of the three options are acceptable.

10. Other Forms of Validation

While this book only covers Column validation formulas and List/Library Item validation formulas, there are a few other options that you may want to research.

Validation Options

Data entry validation can be performed in several places:

- Column validation formulas
- List/Library Item validation formulas
- Custom JavaScript added to a page
- JSLink
- Field Customizer Extensions
- Custom InfoPath forms
- Custom ASPX forms
- Workflows

Each of these have a few shortcomings:

- Column validation formulas.
    - Only validates the current column with no reference to other columns.
    - Does not support JavaScript or Regular Expressions.
    - Does not validate against other items in the list.
- List/Library Item validation formulas.
    - Does not support JavaScript or Regular Expressions.

- o   Does not validate against other items in the list.
- Custom JavaScript added to a page.
  - o   Developer skills needed.
  - o   Probably will not work in the next version of SharePoint.
- JSLink.
  - o   Developer skills needed.
  - o   SharePoint 2013 and later.
  - o   Not supported in Events (calendar) and Survey lists.
  - o   Not supported in the "modern UI" in SharePoint 2016, 2019 and SharePoint Online, but still works in the "classic UI".
  - o   Being replaced in the "modern UI" with "Field Customizer Extensions". https://docs.microsoft.com/en-us/sharepoint/dev/spfx/extensions/get-started/building-simple-field-customizer
- Field Customizer Extensions.
  - o   Not supported in the "classic UI".
- Custom InfoPath forms.
  - o   Not supported in the "modern UI" in SharePoint 2016, 2019 and SharePoint Online, but still works in the "classic UI".
  - o   InfoPath is "deprecated" and is no longer being updated, but will still work in the "classic UI".
- Custom ASPX forms.
  - o   Developer skills needed.
- Workflows.
  - o   Workflow skills needed.
  - o   Workflows are asynchronous and run after the item has been saved or changed.

11. **Workflow Workarounds**

Calculated columns and Validation columns do not work with all SharePoint column types. As a workaround, a SharePoint Designer workflow can often be used to copy the data from the unsupported column types to supported column types.

Unsupported columns in SharePoint formulas:

- Lookup columns.
- Multivalued columns. For example: Choice columns with the "checkboxes" option enabled.
- Multiple lines of text columns.
- Person or Group columns. (These have two values: display name and user ID.)
- Hyperlink columns. (These have two values: display text, and the URL.)
- Managed Metadata columns.
- Hidden columns. Internal columns used by SharePoint.

Some of these are a bit more complicated than they first appear as they contain multiple pieces of data. A Single Line of Text or a Number column will simply store the expected value. Workflows will often let us pick one of these values, and can often retrieve data that's not stored directly in the column.

- **Person or Group** (Examples in a Task list: Assigned To, Created By and Modified By)
    - o As seen from PowerShell or code:
       i:0#.w|spdemo\samc
    - o A workflow can also expose the user's Display Name, Email Address, Login Name and User Id Number. SPD 2010 workflows can also get the user's manager. SPD 2013 workflows can call REST web services and get any of the user's User Profile properties.
- **Choice column with checkboxes**. (Here the user selected Green and Blue from a list of colors.)
    - o As seen from PowerShell or code:
       ;#Green;#Blue;#
        - ▪ Note that the result is just a string with delimiters. (;#)

151

- A workflow can return the list of choices are a simple string:
  Green,Blue
  - You can then apply a Calculated Column's formula to format and display the choices
  - SPD2013 workflows can also manipulate and count the individual selections.
- **Hyperlink**
  - As seen from PowerShell or code:
    http://www.bing.com, Search Bing   (The URL, and the display text.)
  - Workflows can return the string above, the Display Text or the URL.
- **Metadata**
  - **Appliances|f6004674-a3fc-46f3-878f-99512e5e3e22**
    The display text and the unique Identifier (GUID) for the term.
  - Workflows can return the string above, the Display Text or the URL.
- **Multiple Lines of Text**
  - <div class="ExternalClass10D6B9A57E5C4433A96B042A80931439">
    <p><strong>Hello</strong></p><p>World!</p></div>
    (The HTML of the formatted test.)
  - Workflows can return the string above (the HTML version or a plain text version.

Workflow Notes and Tips

For this book, we will only explore SharePoint Designer Workflows to create workarounds for a few Calculated Column shortcomings. We will cover just enough of SharePoint Designer workflows to solve a few of these simple problems.

Please review these workflow notes before proceeding:

- SharePoint Designer 2013 is used to create workflows for SharePoint 2013, 2016, 2019 and SharePoint Online. SharePoint Designer 2010 is used to create workflows for SharePoint 2010.
- SharePoint Designer is free and can be downloaded from Microsoft.
  - SharePoint Designer 2010:
    https://www.microsoft.com/en-us/download/details.aspx?id=16573
  - SharePoint Designer 2013:
    https://www.microsoft.com/en-us/download/details.aspx?id=35491
- Your SharePoint administrators may have blocked the use of SharePoint Designer with your SharePoint farm or with your SharePoint Site Collection.
- SharePoint Designer 2013 supports two styles of workflows:
  - Platform Type: SharePoint 2010 Workflow (*We will use "SPD2010 workflow" to refer to these workflows in the rest of the chapter.*)
    - Often the easier and most complete version to use.

- Available on all SharePoint versions from 2013 on.
- Workflow permissions are either those of the current user, or the user who created the workflow (using Impersonation Steps).

o **Platform Type: SharePoint 2013 Workflow** (*We will use "SPD2013 workflow" to refer to these workflows in the rest of the chapter.*)

- Is missing a number of the SPD2010 Actions and features. You can use REST web service calls to replace most of these.
- Offers REST web service calls to let you access a lot more of SharePoint including other lists, sites and features. REST is more complex than the built-in SPD2010 Actions, but far more powerful.
- Workflow permissions are either the current user, or configured using "App" permissions (using App Steps and additional site level configuration).

- SPD2013 workflows can call SPD2010 workflows, but not the other way around.
- Workflows are asynchronous and may be executed anywhere from almost immediately to minutes after the list item was updated. You may need to refresh the page or reload the list to see the changes.
- Workflows can fail to run. Check the list's workflow history to check the status of a workflow or contact your SharePoint administrator and ask them to check for workflow issues.
- Workflows are not easy to debug. You can add Log to History List workflow actions to log progress messages and the values of variables as they change.

Common Workflow Steps

To avoid repeating the same content over and over, we'll list here some of the common workflow steps that are used in most of the examples that follow.

Creating a Workflow

1. Open SharePoint Designer and connect to your site.
2. In the **Navigation** section click **Workflows**.
3. From the ribbon click **List Workflow** and select your list.

List
Workflow ▾

4. Give the workflow a name and select either "**SharePoint 2010 Workflow**" or "**SharePoint 2013 Workflow**". Note that some of the examples in this chapter will only work with one of these

options.

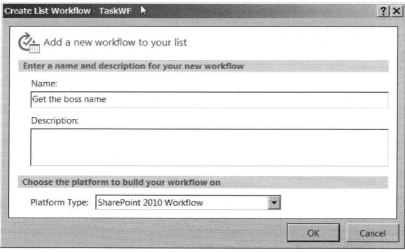

5. Click **OK**.

Completing and Publishing a Workflow

1. SPD2013 only: 2013 style workflows require a formal exit and must "transition" to an "End of workflow".

   a. In your last stage, click in the Transition to stage area.
   b. From the Action ribbon button select Go to stage.
   c. Click the "a stage" link and click End of Workflow.

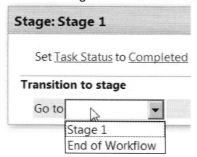

2. Click **Workflow Settings** in the ribbon.

Workflow
Settings

3.   In the **Start Settings** section configure the workflow to start when the item is created or edited.

> ### Start Options
>
> Change the start options for this workflow.
>
> ☑ Allow this workflow to be manually started
>
>   ☐ Require Manage List permissions
>
> ☑ Start workflow automatically when an item is created
>
> ☑ Start workflow automatically when an item is changed

The "manually" option is good for testing, but not required for all of the examples in this chapter.

4.   Click **Publish** in the ribbon.

Publish

Checking the Status of a Workflow

When first run, a workflow will add a column to the list with the same name as the workflow. You can remove these columns from your views. These columns display the status of the workflow, and for 2013 workflows, the name of the last stage processed. Unless changed by your SharePoint administrator, workflow logs are kept for 60 days.

Calc Wholesale Price

Completed

To see the status of the workflow either click the link in the workflow column or select the row and in the ITEMS/DOCUMENTS ribbon click the Workflow icon. From this page you can start workflows and see a list of running and completed workflows.

Start a New Workflow

 Calc Wholesale Price

Workflows (Workflow Health)

Select a workflow to view more details.   Show my workflows only.

Name   Started

Running Workflows

There are no running workflows on this item.

Completed Workflows

Calc Wholesale Price   1/22/2018 7:19 PM

Status of a workflow:

Workflow Status: Calc Wholesale Price

Workflow Information

Initiator: Administrator   **Item:**   Desktop Computer
Started: 1/22/2018 7:19 PM   **Status:** Completed
Last run: 1/22/2018 7:19 PM

⬅ The status, or an error icon will be displayed here.

Information about this instance will be automatically removed on 3/23/2018 8:19 PM.

Tasks ⬅ Any tasks created by the workflow will be listed here.

This workflow created the following tasks. You can also view them in Tasks 1.

| ☐ | Assigned To | Title | Due Date | Status | Related Content |

There are no items to show in this view of the "Tasks 1" list. To add a new item, click "New".

Workflow History ⬅ "Log to History List" message will be listed here.

The workflow recorded these events.

☐	Date Occurred	Event Type	User ID	Description
	1/22/2018 7:19 PM	Comment	☐ System Account	Workflow started

A workflow with an error:

156

Item: Road-150 Red, 62

Internal Status: Suspended

Status: Stage 1

> Resume this workflow
> RequestorId: 0bb0676e-8bd6-2351-0000-
> 000000000000. Details: An unhandled exception
> occurred during the execution of the workflow
> instance. Exception details:
> System.IO.InvalidDataException: Unable to
> deserialize HTTP response content. Expected

Debugging a Workflow

SharePoint Designer workflows have little in the way of debugging tools. You can write messages to a column or to the workflow log. The Log to History List action is usually the best approach as the messages stay hidden from the end user of the list.

When creating the log message, you can type text directly in the Action or click the "…" to open the String Builder to create messages with text and one or more variables and column values.

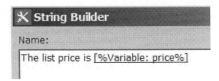

The result might look like this:

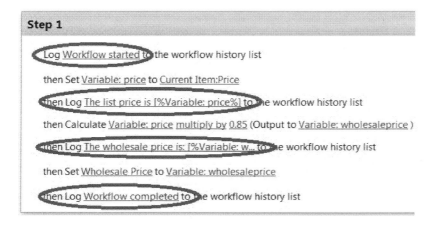

The workflow's log would then include this Workflow History:

Workflow History

The workflow recorded these events.

Date Occurred	Event Type	User ID	Description
1/22/2018 7:19 PM	Comment	System Account	Workflow started
1/22/2018 7:19 PM	Comment	System Account	The list price is 1000
1/22/2018 7:19 PM	Comment	System Account	The wholesale price is: 850
1/22/2018 7:19 PM	Comment	System Account	Workflow completed

Workaround for People and Groups

Your first reason for looking at workflows with a Person or Group column will probably be to just copy the user's name into a Single Line of Text column so it can be used with a Calculated Column. Workflows can actually extract four different user properties. SPD2010 workflows can also return the user's manager name!

The data stored in a People and Groups column is relatively simple, just the internal ID and the display name of the user. A SharePoint Designer workflow can take that raw data and return four user properties:

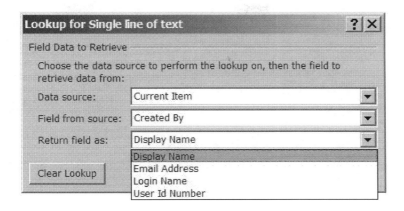

- The "Return field as" **As String** and **Login Name** options both return a two part string that includes the authentication being used and the user's login.

  i:0#.w|spdemo\susanj

  The login name has two parts: the authentication technique and the user's login name.

  - ○ "i:0#.w" is the code for "Windows Authentication". This prefix to login names was needed after SharePoint started supporting Claims Based Authentication. In theory, you could have two "spdemo\samc" users, each authenticated using a different Claims provider. For details see:
    https://social.technet.microsoft.com/wiki/contents/articles/13921.sharepoint-20102013-claims-encoding.aspx
  - ○ "spdemo\susanj" is the domain name for the user.
- **Display Name** is the first and last name of the user. (The actual text and format may vary based on your Active Directory or other authentication provider configuration.)

  Susan Jones
- The **User Id Number** is a number unique to a Site Collection. The same user may have different ID numbers in each Site Collection.
- The Email Address is, well, an email address!

  susanj@example.com

Here's an example workflow using just four **Set Field in Current Item** workflow actions to display data about a user in four Single Line of Text columns:

Step 1

Set <u>Display Name</u> to <u>Current Item:Sales Manager</u>

then Set <u>Email Address</u> to <u>Current Item:Sales Manager</u>

then Set <u>Login Name</u> to <u>Current Item:Sales Manager</u>

then Set <u>User ID Number</u> to <u>Current Item:Sales Manager</u>

And here's the result after running the workflow:

Sales Manager	Display Name	Email Address	Login Name	User ID Number
☐ Sam Conklin	Sam Conklin	samc@spdemo.com	i:0#.w|spdemo\samc	9

If you wanted just the Login Name without the Claims information then:

- Add a Calculated column that uses the workflow above and a formula something like this:
  =MID([Login Name], FIND("|", [Login Name]) + 1, 99)
  To deal with an empty column or with logins without Claims data:
  =IF(ISNUMBER(FIND("|", [Login Name])),
      MID([Login Name], FIND("|", [Login Name]) + 1, 99), "")
  or
- In a SPD2013 workflow, use the **Find Substring in String** action to find the location of the "|" in the data, add a **Do Calculation** action to create a new variable that will be one greater than the location of the "|" and then use the **Extract Substring from Index of String** action to copy everything after the "|".

Two People and Groups examples follow:

- Getting Data from a Person or Group Column
- Getting a User's Manager

Getting Data from a People or Group Column

This is a simple one Action workflow that simply copies the Display Name value from a People and Group column into a Single Line of Text column.

Steps:

1. This example uses a task list with these columns:

     a.   **Boss** (a Person or Group column)

     b.   **Boss Name** (a Single Line of Text)

2.   See "Common Workflow Steps" for starting a workflow. Select either "**SharePoint 2010 Workflow**" or "**SharePoint 2013 Workflow**". (They both have the same "Set Field" action.)

3.   In the workflow add a **Set Field in Current Item** action.

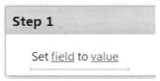

4.   Click **field** and select **Boss Name**.

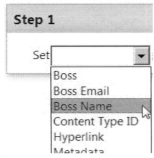

5.   Click **value**.

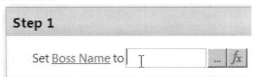

6.   Click the ***fx*** button and select "**Current Item**", "**Boss**" and "**Display Name**".

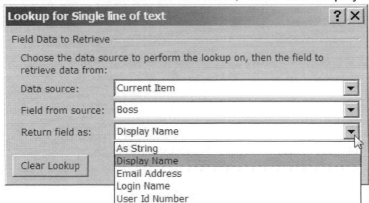

7.   Your workflow could update other fields or perform other actions… but we are going to let this one just update the boss's name.

8. Here's the complete workflow!

> **Step 1**
>
> Set Boss Name to Current Item:Boss

9. See "Common Workflow Steps" for completing and publishing a workflow.
10. Return to your list and make some changes to the Boss column and confirm that the Boss Name column is being updated.
    a. Note that workflows are asynchronous and run in the background. You may need to refresh the page or reselect the view to display the updates.

11. You can now create a Calculated column that uses the boss's name.
    a. Add a new column to the list.
    b. Name it "**Message**".
    c. Make it a Calculated column.
    d. Enter a formula to use the boss's name.
       = "For more info contact " & [Boss Name]
    e. Save the new column and test.

12. The columns should look something like this:

Boss	Boss Name	GetBossInfo	Message
☐ Susan Jones	Susan Jones	Completed	For more info contact Susan Jones

13. Modify the view and remove the Boss, Boss Name and the workflow status column (GetBossIfno).

Task	Message
Plan the Qtrly Mtg	For more info contact Susan Jones

When you add or edit an item in this list you will not see the calculated columns listed, but you will see the "Boss" column the extra columns we added to hold the results of the workflow.

Boss	Susan Jones x │
Boss Name	

Save   Cancel

You can either customize the New and Edit forms using InfoPath or SharePoint Designer to hide these fields, or just add a Description to the extra columns to let the users know that they will be auto-populated.

Boss Name	

This field is auto-populated.

Getting a User's Manager

While the previous example works nicely, we had to enter the boss's name. As you are exploring SharePoint Designer workflows, you should take a look at the "Lookup Manager of a User" action. This action is only available in SPD 2010 workflows, but can be emulated in SPD 2013 workflows by using a REST web service call. The use of this action will require a "well maintained Active Directory" that contains up to date manager data!

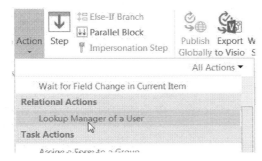

Notes:

- The "Lookup Manager of a User" action is only available from SPD2010 workflows.
- If using SPD2013 workflows, you can use the following REST call get a user's manager:
  http://*server/sites/yourSite/*
  _api/SP.UserProfiles.PeopleManager/
  GetUserProfilePropertyFor(accountName=@v,propertyName='*Manager*')
  ?@v='*spdemo\samc*'
    o The above is all one line.
    o The "v=" value is the user's login name.
    o The "propertyName" could also be any property from User Profile Services. For example:
      propertyName='WorkPhone'

Steps:

1. This example uses a list with these columns:
   a. **Boss Name** (a Single Line of Text)
2. See "Common Workflow Steps" for starting a workflow. Select "**SharePoint 2010 Workflow**". (Only the 2010 version has the Lookup Manager action.)

3. Add the **Lookup Manager of a User** action.

   Find Manager of this user (output to Variable: manager)

4. Click **this user**.
   Select the column that contains the user: ("**Assigned To**" in this example.)

    a.   In the **Select User** dialog click **Workflow Lookup for a User**… and click the **Add >>** button.

    b.   Select **Current Item, Assigned To, Login Names, Semicolon Delimited.**

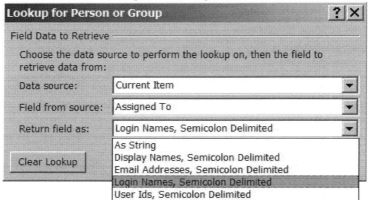

Note: Selecting "Display Names" option will not work. You must use "Login Names".

    c.   Click **OK** and **OK**.

5.   We will leave the "manager" variable name for now, but you could change it if you like.

6.   Add the **Set Field in Current Item** action.

> then Set field to value

7.   Click **field** and select **Boss Name.**

8.   Click **value** and click **_fx_**.

9.   Select **Workflow Variables and Parameters, Variable: manager** and **Display Name**, and click **OK**.

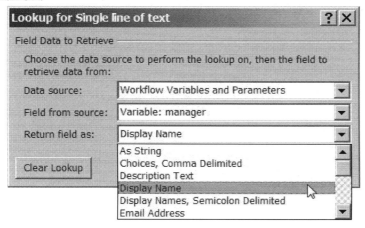

10. Here's the complete workflow!

> ### Step 1
>
> Find Manager of <u>Current Item:Assigned To</u> (output to <u>Variable: manager</u>)
>
> then Set <u>Boss Name</u> to <u>Variable: manager</u>

11. Click **Workflow Settings** in the ribbon.

Workflow
Settings

12. In the **Start Settings** section configure the workflow to start when the item is created or edited.

> ### Start Options
>
> Change the start options for this workflow.
>
> ☑ Allow this workflow to be manually started
> ☐ Require Manage List permissions
> ☑ Start workflow automatically when an item is created
> ☑ Start workflow automatically when an item is changed

The "manually" option is good for testing, but not required for this example.

13. Click **Publish** in the ribbon.

Publish

14. Return to your list and make some changes to the **Assigned To** column and confirm that the **Boss Name** column is being updated.
    a. Note that workflows are asynchronous and run in the background. You may need to refresh the page or reselect the view to display the updates.

The steps that follow are basically the same as the previous example.

15. You can now create a Calculated column that uses the boss's name.
    a. Add a new column to the list.
    b. Name it "**Message**".
    c. Make it a Calculated column.
    d. Enter a formula to use the boss's name.
       = "For more info contact " & [Boss Name]
    e. Save the new column and test.

16. The columns should look something like this:

Boss Name	GetBossInfo	Message
Susan Jones	Completed	For more info contact Susan Jones

17. Modify the view and remove the **Boss**, **Boss Name** and the workflow status column (GetBossIfno).

Task	Message
Plan the Qtrly Mtg	For more info contact Susan Jones

When you add or edit an item in this list you will not see the calculated columns listed in the New and Edit forms, but you will see the "Boss" column and the extra column we added to hold the results of the workflow. You can either customize the New and Edit forms using InfoPath or SharePoint Designer, or just add a Description to the extra columns to let the users know that they will be auto-populated.

Boss Name

This field is auto-populated.

Workaround for the SUBSTITUTE Function

SharePoint formulas do not support the Excel text "search and replace" function. With a little work we can use the SharePoint 2013 workflow's Replace Substring in String action to do what the SUBSTITUTE function does.

A simple example: replace dashes with spaces.

Many files imported into SharePoint libraries from network shares have underlines and dashes in their names. To improve the appearance of these names you might add a Calculated Column with a formula to replace these characters with spaces. This would be easy if SharePoint formulas supported the SUBSTITUTE function. As it does not, we can turn to a SharePoint 2013 style workflow that has a similar capability. While a workflow could just clean up the file name itself, we may have business reasons to not change the original name of the file. Here we will just use the workflow to copy the file name, without the symbols, to a Single Line of Text column.

	Name		File Name
	01_WSS_CPI_Whitepaper	•••	01 WSS CPI Whitepaper
	1 what new SP2013	•••	1 what new SP2013
	2017_Annual_Budget	•••	2017 Annual Budget

Steps:

1. This example uses a Document library with these columns:
   a. **File Name** (a Single Line of Text column)
   b. The default **Name** column.
2. We have a few documents with underlines in their names such as "2017_Annual_Budget.xlsx".
3. See "Common Workflow Steps" for starting a workflow. Select "**SharePoint 2013 Workflow**".

4. From the **Utility Actions** section of the **Action** ribbon button click **Replace substring in string.**
5. Click **string** and enter the character to replace, "_" for this example.
6. Click the next string placeholder and enter a single space. (this will display as a short underline)

   Replace _ with _ in string (Output to Variable: output)
7. Click the third string placeholder and select the column that contains the string with the unwanted underlines; "Name" in this example.

   Replace _ with _ in Current Item:Name (Output to Variable: output)
8. You can enter your own variable name, or leave the "output" name.
9. To replace any additional characters, such as a dash ("-"), add another Replace action to update the "output" variable.

   Replace _ with _ in Current Item:Name (Output to Variable: output)

   then Replace - with _ in Variable: output (Output to Variable: output)

10. Finally, update the Single Line of Text column you added with the value of the "output" variable. "File Name" in this example.

    then Set File Name to Variable: output
11. Set the **Transition to stage** to go to the **End of Workflow**.
12. The final workflow should look like this:

Stage: Stage 1

Replace _ with _ in Current Item:Name (Output to Variable: output)

then Replace - with _ in Variable: output (Output to Variable: output)

then Set File Name to Variable: output

Transition to stage

Go to End of Workflow

---

13. In the **Start Settings** section configure the workflow to start when the item is created or edited.

Start Options

Change the start options for this workflow.

☑ Allow this workflow to be manually started
     ☐ Require Manage List permissions
☑ Start workflow automatically when an item is created
☑ Start workflow automatically when an item is changed

The "manually" option is good for testing, but not required for this example.

14. Click **Publish** in the ribbon.

Publish

15. Return to your list and test.

A SUBSTITUE example to encode a Query String value

To create more complex search and replace workflows, just keep adding **Replace substring in string actions**. URLs have a list of special characters such as "?", "&" and "=", which if included with data in the query string part of the URL, can cause issues. These can be replaced with encoded values.

For example, if you have these columns in your list:

ProductID: 123

RequestedDocument: Q&A Report

You might try to build a Calculated Column with this formula:

="http://someDomain/product.aspx?ProductID=" & ProductID &
   "&Document=" & RequestedDocument

Which will create this result:

http://someDomain/product.aspx?ProductID=123&Document=**Q&A Report**

The "&" and the space in "Q&A" will not be correctly processed by the product.aspx page and will result in an error or the wrong data. The solution is to replace all the problem characters with an encoding acceptable in URLs. For example, a space can be encoded as "%20" and the "&" character can be encoded as "%26".

If we wanted to create something like this:

ProductID	RequestedDocument	ProductLink
123	Q&A Report	http://someDomain/product.aspx?ProductID=123&Document=Q%26A%20Report
1234	Sales Report 12	http://someDomain/product.aspx?ProductID=1234&Document=Sales%20Report%2012

We will need:

- A ProductID column (Single line of text)
- A RequestedDocument column (Single line of text)
- A ProductLink column (Hyperlink or Picture)
  Note: If the output of this workflow will be used by a Calculated Column, save the result to a Single Line of Text column instead of a Hyperlink column.
- A workflow!

The workflow might look like this:

Stage: Stage 1

Set Variable: text to Current Item:RequestedDocument   Save the document name to a variable

then Replace ? with %3F in Variable: text (Output to Variable: text)

then Replace % with %25 in Variable: text (Output to Variable: text)

then Replace _ with %20 in Variable: text (Output to Variable: text)

then Replace & with %26 in Variable: text (Output to Variable: text)

then Replace = with %3D in Variable: text (Output to Variable: text)

then Replace { with %7B in Variable: text (Output to Variable: text)   Do the needed replacements

then Replace } with %7D in Variable: text (Output to Variable: text)

then Replace [with %5B in Variable: text (Output to Variable: text)

then Replace] with %5D in Variable: text (Output to Variable: text)

then Replace - with %2D in Variable: text (Output to Variable: text)

then Set Variable: HyperLinkString to http://someDomain/product.aspx?Produc...   Create the URL and save it back to the hyperlink column

then Set ProductLink to Variable: HyperLinkString

Transition to stage

Go to End of Workflow

The String Builder for the URL looks like this:

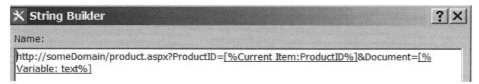

Tip! To create a hyperlink that displays text instead of the URL just add a comma and the display text!

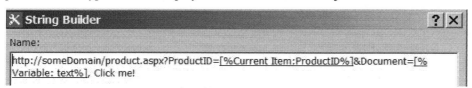

Workaround for Getting View Totals from Calculated Columns.

It seems that the folks who created views forgot something. While views can display, group by, sort and filter on Calculated columns, they cannot total those columns.

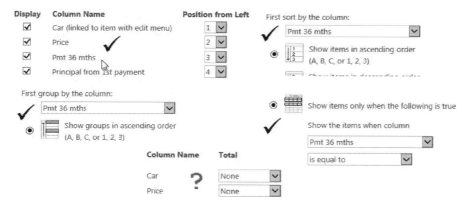

All we need to do to work around this problem is to have a workflow copy the value of the Calculated Column into a Number column.

Workaround for Adding Images to a Column

Calculated columns cannot interact with Hypertext or Picture columns. They can neither display an image or read a value from a Hypertext or Picture column. Workflows can set the URLs in a Hypertext or Picture column, and can either contain the logic select the image or use data from a Calculated Column to select the image.

In this example:

- We are using three images named KPIDefault-0, KPIDefault-1 and KPIDefault-2. (Green, Yellow, Red)
- These sample images are found in /_layouts/images. These images are supplied with SharePoint, but you could use your own images stored in any library.
- We are displaying:
  - 100% complete as green.
  - 0% complete as red.
  - Anything else as yellow.

Here's what the workflow looks like:

Step 1

Set Variable: ImageName to KPIDefault-1.GIF

If Current Item:% Complete equals 1

    Set Variable: ImageName to KPIDefault-0.GIF

Else if Current Item:% Complete equals 0

    Set Variable: ImageName to KPIDefault-2.GIF

then Set Variable: ImageURL to http://sp2016/_layouts/images/[%Varia...

then Set TaskImage to Variable: ImageURL

Steps:

1. This example uses a Task list with these columns:
   a. **% Complete** (a Number column)
   b. **TaskImage** (a Hyperlink or Picture column)

2. See "Common Workflow Steps" for starting a workflow. Select either "**SharePoint 2010 Workflow**" or "**SharePoint 2013 Workflow**". (They both have the same "Set Field" action.)

3. From the **Core Actions** section of the **Action** ribbon button click **Set Workflow Variable**.
4. Click **workflow variable** and enter a name. ("ImageName" was used in this example.)
5. Click **value** and enter the name of your default image. ("KPIDefault-1.GIF" in this example. It's a yellow icon.)
6. Just below the previous action add an **If any value equals any value** Condition.

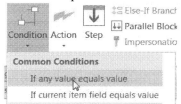

7. Click the first **value** and click ***fx***.
8. Select **Current Item** and the column that contains your test value. ("% Complete" in this example.)

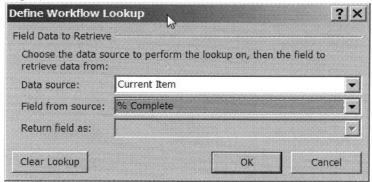

9. Click **OK**.
10. For this example we will use the "equals" operator. You selection will depend on your data.
11. Click the second **value** and click ***fx***.
12. Type "**1**" and **OK**. (1 = 100% complete.)

> If <u>Current Item:% Complete</u> <u>equals</u> <u>1</u>
>
>   (Start typing or use the Insert group on the Ribbon.)

13. Click in the area below the IF and from the **Core Actions** section of the **Action** ribbon button select **Set Workflow Variable**.
14. Click **workflow variable** and select the variable name we used earlier. ("ImageName" in this example.)
15. Click **value** and enter the name of your default image. ("KPIDefault-0.GIF" in this example. It's a green icon.)

16. Repeat steps 10 – 19 to add another IF block that tests for % Complete = 0 and sets the ImageName variable to "KPIDefault-2.GIF". (This is a red icon)

17. For your projects you may need to add additional IF blocks for each additional icon you might display.

18. In the steps above we only stored the image name in a variable. Now we need to add to that name the full URL to the image.

19. Click in the area below the IF and from the Core Actions section of the Action ribbon button select Set Workflow Variable.

20. Click workflow variable and select Create a new variable.

21. Enter a new variable name ("ImageURL" for this example), set the type to String and click OK.

22. Click value and click ...

23. In the String Builder window type the path to the library where you have stored the images, or in this example the path to the SharePoint default images. These might look like:

   http://*yourServer/sites/yourSite*/_layouts/images/

   or

   http://*yourServer/sites/yourSite*/SiteAssets/

   or

   http://*yourServer/sites/yourSite*/yourDocumentLibrary/

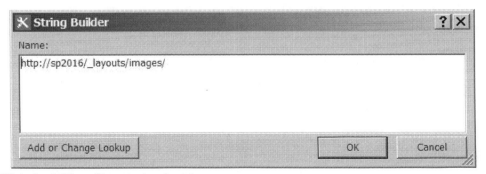

24. Click the Add or Change Lookup button.

25. Select **Workflow Variables and Parameters, Variable: ImageURL** (or your variable name) and
    As String.

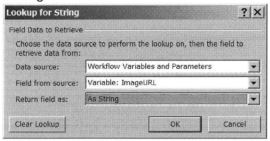

26. Click **OK**.

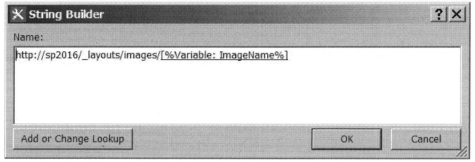

27. Click OK.
28. From the **Action** ribbon button select **Set Field in Current Item**.
29. Click **field** and pick your Hyperlink or Picture column. ("TaskImage" for this example.)
30. Click **value** and click **fx**.
31. Select **Workflow Variables and Parameters, Variable: ImageURL** and **As String**.

32. Click OK.
33. Click **Workflow Settings** in the ribbon.

Workflow
Settings

34. In the **Start Settings** section configure the workflow to start when the item is created or edited.

> ### Start Options
>
> Change the start options for this workflow.
>
> ☑ Allow this workflow to be manually started
>
>   ☐ Require Manage List permissions
>
> ☑ Start workflow automatically when an item is created
>
> ☑ Start workflow automatically when an item is changed

The "manually" option is good for testing, but not required for this example.

35. Click **Publish** in the ribbon.

Publish

36. Return to your task list and enter a few sample tasks and verify that the correct icons or pictures are being displayed.

Here's the result:

Task Name		Due Date	% Complete	Task Status	TaskImage
Plan the Trade Show	•••		50 %	In Progress	△
Create event budget ✶	•••		100 %	Completed	●
Order candy bowl! ✶	•••		0 %	Not Started	◆
Schedule table staff ✶	•••		20 %	In Progress	△
Schedule travel and hotel ✶	•••		0 %	Not Started	◆

Workaround for Multiple Lines of Text

To create a column from a Multiple Lines of Text column we need to pick the characters to copy and then only up to 255 characters. If the column is of type Rich or Enhanced, then we need to copy just the plain text version and not the HTML.

Notes:

- Only the first 255 characters can be copied from a Multiple Lines of Text column to a Single Line of Text column.

175

- There are workflow actions available to extract "x" characters from the beginning of the text, "x" characters from the end of the text, all characters from position "x" to the end, or "y" characters starting at position "y".

  Utility Actions

  Extract Substring from End of String

  Extract Substring from Index of String

  Extract Substring from Start of String

  Extract Substring of String from Index with Length

- SPD2013 workflows seem to ignore the "Plain text" option and always return the HTML tags from the Multiple Lines of Text column. So… create this one as a SPD2010 workflow.

The Workflow:

Step 1

Copy 255 characters from start of Current Item:MultiLines (Output to Variable: substring)

then Log Text copied: [%Variable: substring%] to the workflow history list

then Set MultiResult to Variable: substring

Steps:

1. See "Common Workflow Steps" for starting a workflow. Select either "SharePoint 2010 Workflow" or "SharePoint 2013 Workflow".

2. From the Utility section of the Action ribbon button click Extract Substring from Start of String or one of the other extracts depending on your data.

   Utility Actions

   Extract Substring from End of String

   Extract Substring from Index of String

   Extract Substring from Start of String

   Extract Substring of String from Index with Length

   Find Interval Between Dates

3. Change the 0 to 255.
4. Click string and click *fx*.

5. Select **Current Item**, your Multiple Line of Text field, and **Plain Text** and click **OK**.

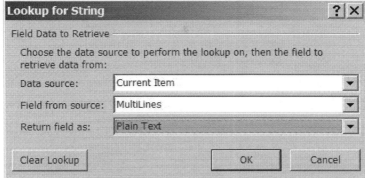

Note: if you select **String** you will also copy any HTML tags from the column.

6. You can change the "**substring**" variable name if you like. We will leave the default name for this example.
7. Directly below the previous Action, add a **Set Field in Current Item** Action.
8. Click **field** and select your destination Single Line of Text column. (**MultiResult** in this example.)
9. Click **value** and click *fx*.
10. Select **Workflow Variables and Parameters**, your new variable (**substring** in this example) and **Plain Text**.

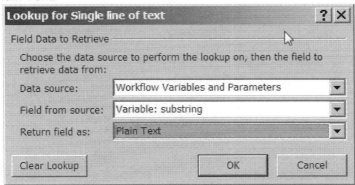

11. Click **OK**.
12. Click **Workflow Settings** in the ribbon.

Workflow
Settings

13. In the **Start Settings** section configure the workflow to start when the item is created or edited.

Start Options

Change the start options for this workflow.

- ☑ Allow this workflow to be manually started
    - ☐ Require Manage List permissions
- ☑ Start workflow automatically when an item is created
- ☑ Start workflow automatically when an item is changed

The "manually" option is good for testing, but not required for this example.

14. Click **Publish** in the ribbon.

Publish

15. Return to your list, add a new item with more than 255 characters in the Multiple Lines of Text column and save your changes.

16. You may need to refresh the page or redisplay the list to see the changes.

MultiLines

To create a column from a Multiple Lines of Text column we need to pick the characters to copy and only up to 255 characters. To create a column from a Multiple Lines of Text column we need to pick the characters to copy and only up to 255 characters. To create a column from a Multiple Lines of Text column we need to pick the characters to copy and only up to 255 characters. To create a column from a Multiple Lines of Text column we need to pick the characters to copy and only up to 255 characters.

MultiResult

To create a column from a Multiple Lines of Text column we need to pick the characters to copy and only up to 255 characters. To create a column from a Multiple Lines of Text column we need to pick the characters to copy and only up to 255 characters. To

17. You now have a column that can be referenced by a Calculated column.

Workaround for Lookup Columns

The workflow workaround for Lookup Columns is similar to the other workarounds in that we copy the text from the lookup column to a Single Line of Text column. We can then use that column in Calculated Column formulas. Lookup Columns also have a multiple choice (checkboxes) option. Generally, Lookup columns with checkboxes are excluded from View Group and Total features. Although often of little use, we can convert multiple choice Lookup columns into text that can be used with those features.

A "no checkboxes" Lookup column stores its data as an ID number, a semicolon+pound sign delimiter, and then the text. In the following example, the 23 is the ID number in the lookup source list, the ";#" is the delimiter and "Cloud Flyer Sailboat" is the text column selected form the source list.

23;#Cloud Flyer Sailboat

When working with multiple values (checkboxes) the data stored in the Lookup column consists of sets of the above with semicolons as the delimiter.

23;#Cloud Flyer Sailboat;#81;#Silver Arrow Sailboat;#54;#3D Competition Helicopter

When using a workflow, we can convert a single valued Lookup column's value into two possible results "As String" and "Lookup Value (as Text)". The second is often the most useful.

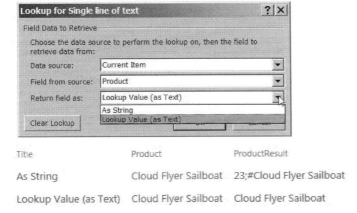

Title	Product	ProductResult
As String	Cloud Flyer Sailboat	23;#Cloud Flyer Sailboat
Lookup Value (as Text)	Cloud Flyer Sailboat	Cloud Flyer Sailboat

When the Lookup column is setup for multiple values (checkboxes) we have three options: "As String", "Lookup Ids, Comma Delimited" and "Lookup Values, Comma Delimited. The third is often the most useful for your Calculated Columns.

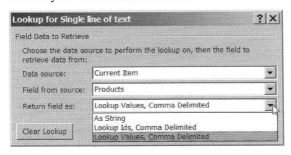

Title	Products	ProductsResult
As String	Cloud Flyer Sailboat; Silver Arrow Sailboat; 3D Competition Helicopter	23;#Cloud Flyer Sailboat;#81;#Silver Arrow Sailboat;#54;#3D Competition Helicopter
Lookup Ids, Comma Delimited	Cloud Flyer Sailboat; Silver Arrow Sailboat; 3D Competition Helicopter	23,81,54
Lookup Values, Comma Delimited	Cloud Flyer Sailboat; Silver Arrow Sailboat; 3D Competition Helicopter	Cloud Flyer Sailboat,Silver Arrow Sailboat,3D Competition Helicopter

You can then use the FIND or SEARCH functions to check the multiple results for a specific value. For an example of this see "Workaround for Multivalued Choice Columns" later in this chapter.

Lookup a Single Item (No checkboxes)

In this example we have these columns:

- **Bike** – a Lookup Column that uses a list named "Bike" and returns data from a column named "Bike".

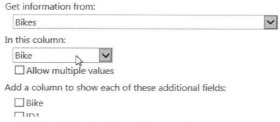

- **FromWF** – A Single Line of Text column that is updated from the workflow. This column can be used by a Calculated column.

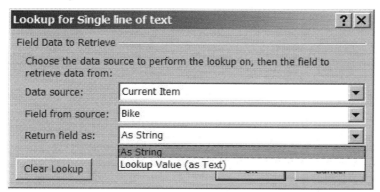

If you retrieve the data as "String" you will get a compound result that includes the ID number of the item in the lookup list. You could use the FIND and MID functions to extract either the ID or the text from this string.

98;#Speed Racer 100

If you retrieve the data as "Lookup Value (as Text)" you will get just the text displayed in the lookup column.

Speed Racer 100

Extract Several Lookup Columns into a Single Line of Text

When you add a Lookup column to a list, you can select additional columns to display in your list. None of these extra columns will be accessible from a Calculated Column. Instead of having the workflow copy each of these values into their own text columns, you can let the workflow create a single value from the combination of looked up columns.

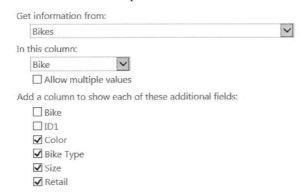

Note:The extra columns will be prefixed with the name of the lookup table. You can edit these columns in the list's properties page and give them cleaner names.

Bike	Lookup
FromWF	Single line of text
Bike:Color	Lookup
Bike:Bike Type	Lookup
Bike:Size	Lookup
Bike:Retail	Lookup

In this example we will build a single string with the column names and the values. You can build the string using the String Builder dialog and using the Add or Change Lookup button to add each column value:

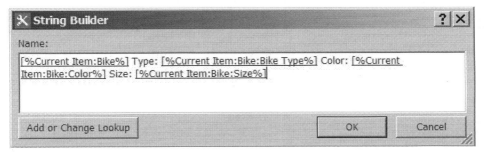

Steps:

1. Create a list with the Lookup Column, with the additional columns that you need checked.
2. Also add a Single Line of Text column to the list to hold the result.
3. See "Common Workflow Steps" for starting a workflow. Select either "**SharePoint 2010 Workflow**" or "**SharePoint 2013 Workflow**". (They both have the same "Set Field" action.)

4. In the workflow add a **Set Field in Current Item** action.

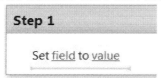

5. Click **field** and select your Single Line of Text file to hold the result.
6. Click **value** and click **...** to display the String Builder dialog box.

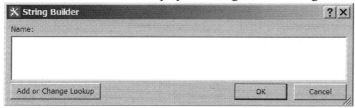

7. Click the **Add or Change Lookup** button.
8. Select **Current Item**, the name of your lookup column, and **Lookup Value (as Text)**.

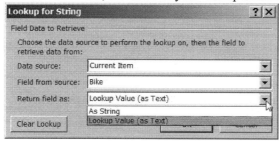

9. Click **OK**.
10. Type any spaces, commas or other text as desired.

11. Repeat steps 11 to 14 as needed to add each additional lookup columns or other columns.

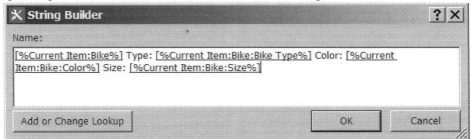

12. Click **OK** to close the String Builder dialog box.
13. Click **Workflow Settings** in the ribbon.

Workflow
Settings

14. In the **Start Settings** section, configure the workflow to start when the item is created or edited.

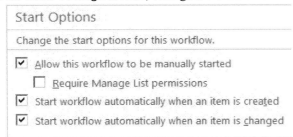

The "manually" option is good for testing, but not required for this example.

15. Click **Publish** in the ribbon.

Publish

16. Return to your list and test.

The original list, without the workflow populated column, looked like this:

Bike	Bike:Color	Bike:Bike Type	Bike:Size
Speed Racer 100	Red	Racer	33

Hiding the lookup columns and just displaying the workflow populated column looks like this:

FromWF

Speed Racer 100 Type: Racer Color: Red Size: 33

Of course, you will want a better column name than "FromWF"!

Workaround for Multivalued Choice Columns

For example: We have a list with a Choice column with the "checkboxes" option enabled that lists options for lunch. We want to use a Calculated Column to validate the lunch order. (Only one entrée please!)

The list looks like this:

Team Member *	Mike
Lunch Choices	☑ Salad ☐ Chicken ☑ Steak ☑ Fries ☑ Pie ☐ Cake
Lunch to Order	
	This field will be populated by a workflow...

Save   Cancel

We need a workflow to copy the multiple choices column into a Single Line of Text column that a Calculated Column can access.

Title		Lunch Choices	Lunch to Order	Get Lunch Order
Test ✻	···	Salad,Steak,Fries,Pie	Salad,Steak,Fries,Pie	Completed

Now that we have that column ("Lunch to Order"), we can write a Calculated Column formula to check to see if someone tried to order both chicken and steak.

```
=IF( AND(
            NOT( ISERROR( FIND( "Steak", [Lunch to Order] ) ) ),
            NOT( ISERROR( FIND( "Chicken", [Lunch to Order] ) ) )
         ),
      "Please only select one entrée",
      "" )
```

Note that the above cannot be used for a Validation formula as the data it needs is not available until after the item has been saved, and the workflow has been run.

The workflow will only need one action and can be written as a 2010 or 2013 style workflow. Add a Set Field in Current Item action and select the data from the Choice column using "Choices, Comma Delimited".

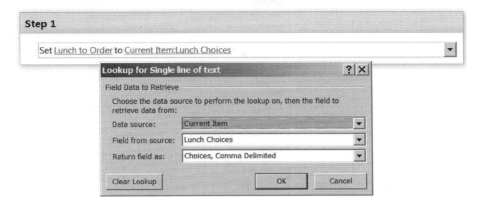

Sam needs to update his order!

Team Member		Lunch Choices	Lunch to Order	Get Lunch Order	Order Check
Mike ✹	•••	Salad,Steak,Fries,Pie	Salad,Steak,Fries,Pie	Completed	
Sam ✹	•••	Salad,Chicken,Steak,Fries,Pie,Cake	Salad,Chicken,Steak,Fries,Pie,Cake	Completed	Please only select one entrée
Susan ✹	•••	Salad,Chicken,Cake	Salad,Chicken,Cake	Completed	

Counting Items Selected in a Multivalued Column

Because SharePoint Calculated Columns cannot work with multivalued columns, they obviously cannot count the number of items selected in one of those columns. So, you cannot do the following with just a Calculated column…

Your Name	Prizes	Message
Mike	3D Competition Helicopter; Cloud Flyer Sailboat	You must select 3 or 5 prizes!
Susan	Cloud Flyer Sailboat; Extra 340 3D; Silver Arrow Sailboat	Thank you!
Sam	3D Competition Helicopter	You must select 3 or 5 prizes!
Richard	3D Competition Helicopter; 3D Sport Helicopter; Cloud Flyer Sailboat; Cloud Flyer Sailboat; Extra 340 3D	Thank you!

With the addition of a little workflow, we can get a count of the choices. While it works, this is not an especially obvious workflow.

How it works:

- This requires features only available in the 2013 version of workflows. (I.e. 2010 will not work!)

185

- This uses three workflow Actions that work with "dictionaries".
  - o **Set Workflow Variable** (from a collection column.)
  - o **Get an Item from a Dictionary**
  - o **Count Items in a Dictionary**
- The first step is to store the collection of values into a variable with a type of Dictionary.

  Set <u>Variable: ValueFromPrizesColumn</u> to <u>Current Item:Products</u>

- This will store the collection of selected items as JavaScript Object Notation (JSON):

  {"results":[{"Id":23,"Value":"Cloud Flyer Sailboat"},
          {"Id":81,"Value":"Silver Arrow Sailboat"},
          {"Id":54,"Value":"3D Competition Helicopter"}]}

- The only problem is that JSON text defines a single object named "results". We need the three items inside of "results". So we use the **Get an Item from a Dictionary** Action to pull out the contents of "results".

  then Get <u>results</u> from <u>Variable: dictionary</u> (Output to <u>Variable: Result</u>)

- This will give us a dictionary with the three items in it.

  [{"Id":23,"Value":"Cloud Flyer Sailboat"},
      {"Id":81,"Value":"Silver Arrow Sailboat"},
      {"Id":54,"Value":"3D Competition Helicopter"}]

- Now we use one more Action, **Count Items in a Dictionary**, to count the items.

  then Count Items in <u>Variable: Result</u> (Output to <u>Variable: count</u>)

- Then all we need to do is write this value back into the list so a Calculated column can pick it up.
- You can then write a Calculated Formula with a message for the user.

  =IF(ISBLANK(PrizeCount),
    "(refresh page for message)",
    IF(OR(PrizeCount=3,PrizeCount=5),
      "Thank you!",
      "You must select 3 or 5 prizes!")
)

Notes:

- ISBLANK checks to see if the number column has a value. It returns True or False. (You may want to come up with a better message!)

Steps:

1. See "Common Workflow Steps" for starting a workflow. Select "**SharePoint 2013 Workflow**". (SPD2010 workflows do not have the features we need for this example.)

2. Add a **Set Workflow Variable** Action.
3. Click workflow variable and create a new variable. For this demo, name it ValueFromPrizesColumn.
4. Click **value** and then ***fx***.
5. Select **Current Item**, your Lookup column and **As Dictionary**.

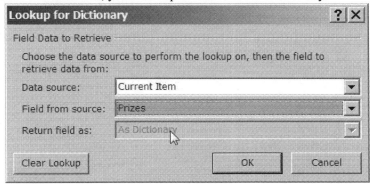

6. Add a **Get an Item from a Dictionary** Action.

    then Get item by name or path from dictionary (Output to item)

7. Click **item by name or path** and enter "results" (no quotes).
8. Click **dictionary** and select the variable you just created.
9. Click **item** and create a new variable named "**PrizeCollection**" and set the type to "**Dictionary**".

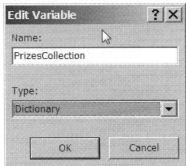

10. Click **OK**.

    then Get results from Variable: ValueFromPrizesColumn (Output to Variable: PrizesCollection)

11. Add a **Count Items in a Dictionary** action.

    then Count Items in dictionary (Output to Variable: count)

12. Click **dictionary** and select the second dictionary variable you created, "**PrizeCollection**".

13. Click **Variable: count** and create a new variable named "**PrizeCount**" and set the type to **Integer**.

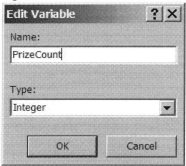

14. Click **OK**.

then Count Items in Variable: PrizesCollection (Output to Variable: PrizeCount)

15. Add a **Set Field in Current Item** Action.

then Set field to value

16. Click **field** and select the column you created for the final count. "**PrizeCount**" in this example.
17. Click **value** and *fx*.
18. Select Workflow Variables and Parameters, Variable: PrizeCount and click **OK**.

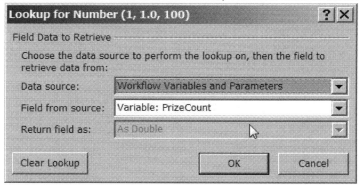

19. Click **Workflow Settings** in the ribbon.

Workflow
Settings

20. In the **Start Settings** section configure the workflow to start when the item is created or edited.

> ### Start Options
> Change the start options for this workflow.
>
> ☑ Allow this workflow to be manually started
>
>   ☐ Require Manage List permissions
>
> ☑ Start workflow automatically when an item is created
>
> ☑ Start workflow automatically when an item is changed

The "manually" option is good for testing, but not required for this example.

21. Click **Publish** in the ribbon.

Publish

22. Return to your list and add a Calculated column to use the count value. Something like this:

```
=IF( ISBLANK(PrizeCount),
   "(refresh page for message)",
   IF( OR( PrizeCount=3, PrizeCount=5 ),
      "Thank you!",
      "You must select 3 or 5 prizes!" )
)
```

23. Test!

Your Name	Prizes	PrizeCount	Message
Mike	3D Competition Helicopter; Cloud Flyer Sailboat	2	You must select 3 or 5 prizes!
Susan	Cloud Flyer Sailboat; Extra 340 3D; Silver Arrow Sailboat	3	Thank you!
Sam	3D Competition Helicopter	0	You must select 3 or 5 prizes!
Richard	3D Competition Helicopter; 3D Sport Helicopter; Cloud Flyer Sailboat; Cloud Flyer Sailboat; Extra 340 3D		(refresh page for message)

Workaround for Managed Metadata columns

Managed Metadata Columns have their own unique formatting and are not directly accessible to Calculated Columns. Even workflows cannot work directly with these columns. Luckily, SharePoint creates an extra column for every Managed Metadata Column that we create. It has the same name, with an "_0" added to the end and contains a text version of the data. This column is also hidden to both Views and Calculated Columns.

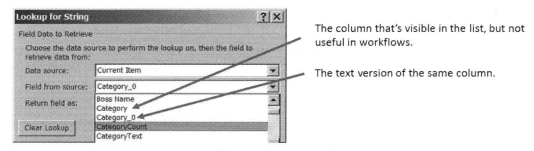

The column that's visible in the list, but not useful in workflows.

The text version of the same column.

The text for a single valued Managed Metadata Column contains the display text for the term and a GUID that uniquely identifies the term in the Managed Metadata Service.

Appliances|f6004674-a3fc-46f3-878f-99512e5e3e22

The text for a multi valued Managed Metadata Column contains a semicolon delimited version of the above.

Appliances|f6004674-a3fc-46f3-878f-99512e5e3e22; **Furniture**|80b90daf-623f-499c-a448-b666055e3f76; **Service**|2dddd18f-66e5-4b3b-a086-d190423a8044

As the "_0" version of the column is only text, it cannot be processed as a workflow dictionary variable.

So what can you do with it?

- Copy the "_0" version of the column to a Single Line of Text column and then use a Calculated column to parse the display text.
- Copy the "_0" version to a workflow variable, use workflow substring actions to extract the display text and then copy the result to a Single Line of Text column.

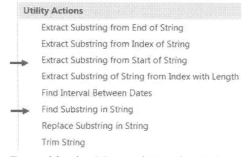

- For multi value Managed Metadata Columns, you could write a workflow loop (SPD2013 only) to count the items or to extract just the display text of the items, and then write the result to a Single Line of Text column.

Workaround for Single Valued Managed Metadata Columns

This example takes the Managed Metadata term stored in a column named "Category" and copies it to a Single Line of Text column so it can be used in a Calculated Column. This example works in both SPD2010 and SPD2013.

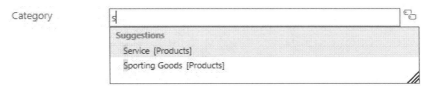

Steps:

1. See "Common Workflow Steps" for starting a workflow. Select either "**SharePoint 2010 Workflow**" or "**SharePoint 2013 Workflow**". (They both have the same "Set Field" action.)

2. In the workflow add a **Set Field in Current Item** Action.

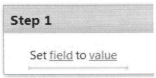

3. Click **field** and select your Single Line of Text column you added to hold the result.
4. Click **value** and click **fx**.
5. Select **Current Item** and the "_0" version of your Managed Metadata column.

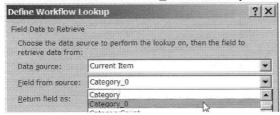

6. Click **OK**.
7. That's it!

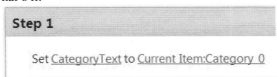

8. Publish and test your workflow as usual!

If you are creating a SPD2013 workflow, then you can let the workflow extract the display text.

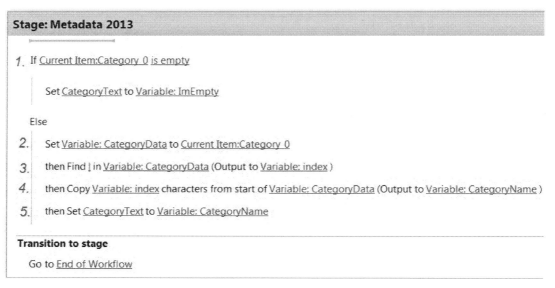

The basic flow is:

1. Check to see if the column is empty, if so, clear any existing value of the output column.
   a. Tip: The **Set Field in Current Item** action will not let you leave the value parameter blank. To blank a column, create a workflow variable (using **Local Variables** in the ribbon), but never set it to anything. In the example above, this is the "**ImEmpty**" variable.
2. Copy the "_0" Managed Metadata column to variable. ("**CategoryData**" above.)
3. Use the **Find Substring in String** Action to locate the vertical bar (|) symbol and store the location into a variable ("**index**").
4. Use the **Extract Substring from Start of String** Action to copy the display name of the term.
5. Use the **Set Field in Current Item** Action to copy the extracted text back to a list column.

Workaround for Multi Valued Managed Metadata Columns

This example counts Managed Metadata terms stored in a column named "Category" and copies count to a Number column so it can be used in a Calculated Column. This example works in only SPD2013 as it uses the 2013 looping features.

Instead of listing pages of steps here, we will just show a summary of the steps needed. While this example counts the terms found in the column, your project may need to extract the text or perform other actions on the data.

Here's the final workflow. The numbers match the steps that follow.

Steps:

1. Create a "SharePoint 2013 Workflow".
2. Copy the text form the "_0" column by adding a **Set Workflow Variable** Action to create string variable to hold the data. (Variable "TheData")
3. Add another **Set Workflow Variable** Action to initialize a counter to zero. ("Variable: Counter")
4. Add an **If any value equals a value** Condition to check to see if there is any data to process.
5. If there is data, initialize the Counter to 1 with another **Set Workflow Variable** Action.
6. Inside of the IF block, add **Loop with Condition** loop that runs as long as there is a ";" in the variable's text.
7. Inside of the loop:

      a. Add a **Do Calculation** Action and a Set Workflow Variable action to add 1 to the counter variable.

      b. Use the **Find Substring in String** Action to find the location of the next ";" in the data.

      c. Add a **Do Calculation** Action to create a new variable that will be one greater than the location of the ";".

      d. Use the **Extract Substring from Index of String** Action to copy everything after the ";".

8. Add a **Set Field in Current Item** Action to copy the counter back into the list so it can be used in a Calculated column, filter or sort.

Workarounds for Attachments

"Attachments" is not a true column, it just displays a paperclip icon if the list item has attachments. It cannot be edited by the user or used in a Calculated Column. There is a list item field available to workflows called "Attachments" that is a Yes/No type that can be checked in a SPD2010 or SPD2013 workflow. A workflow could update a Single Line of Text field with a message or with data to be used with a Calculated Column.

Here we will look at two examples:

- Copy the column to a new column. (SPD2010 and SPD2013)
- Get a count or list of attachments. (SPD2013 only)

Copy the column to a new column. (SPD2010 and SPD2013)

The workaround is very similar to the others you have seen in this chapter, copy the "problem column" to a Single Line of Text column, but with a little twist. Here we will copy the column to a Yes/No column and add a Calculated Column to hold a message.

Title			HasAttachments	More Info
Error on sales report	...	📎	Yes	See attachments for details
Timeout on order entry	...	📎	Yes	See attachments for details
Incorrect tax amount	...			

Steps:

1. This example uses a list with these columns:

      a. **HasAttachments** (a Yes/No column)

2. See "Common Workflow Steps" for starting a workflow. Select either "**SharePoint 2010 Workflow**" or "**SharePoint 2013 Workflow**". (They both have the same "Set Field" action.)

3. In the workflow add a **Set Field in Current Item** Action.

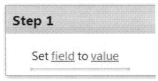

4. Click **field** and select your Single Line of Text column you added to hold the result. "HasAttachments" in this example.
5. Click **value** and click **fx**.
6. Select **Current Item** and **Attachments**.

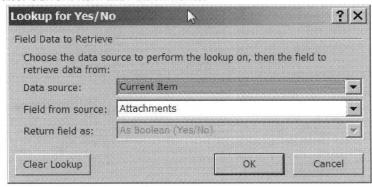

7. The workflow should now look like this:

8. Click **Workflow Settings** in the ribbon.

   Workflow
   Settings

9. In the **Start Settings** section configure the workflow to start when the item is created or edited.

Start Options

Change the start options for this workflow.

☑ Allow this workflow to be manually started
☐ Require Manage List permissions
☑ Start workflow automatically when an item is created
☑ Start workflow automatically when an item is changed

The "manually" option is good for testing, but not required for this example.

10. Click **Publish** in the ribbon.

Publish

11. Now create a Calculated Column to use the HasAttachments column. Maybe something like this:
    =IF([HasAttachments],"See attachments for details","")

Get a count or list of attachments. (SPD2013 only)

SPD2013 workflows can call a SharePoint REST API web service that can get back a list of the attachment files.

http://*yourServer*/sites/*yourSite*/_api/web/lists/getbytitle('*yourList*')/items(1)/AttachmentFiles

You can see what this REST API query does by typing this URL (edited for your site and list of course) into your browser's address bar and pressing Enter.

```
InPrivate      http://yourServer/sites/yourSite/_api/web/lists/getbytitle('yourList')/items(1)/AttachmentFiles

<?xml version="1.0" encoding="utf-8" ?>
- <feed xml:base="http://sp2016/sites/calcdemo/_api/" xmlns="http://www.w3.org/2005/Atom" xmlns:d="F
    xmlns:m="http://schemas.microsoft.com/ado/2007/08/dataservices/metadata" xmlns:georss="http://ww
    <id>4a08ef35-8404-47be-975a-b54b549224a2</id>
    <title />
    <updated>2018-01-11T18:23:39Z</updated>
  - <entry>
      <id>http://sp2016/sites/calcdemo/_api/Web/Lists(guid'd87b7f4b-a43c-410a-8a51-3007f42f0465')/I
      <category term="SP.Attachment" scheme="http://schemas.microsoft.com/ado/2007/08/dataservices/sc
      <link rel="edit" href="Web/Lists(guid'd87b7f4b-a43c-410a-8a51-3007f42f0465')/Items(1)/AttachmentF
      <title />
      <updated>2018-01-11T18:23:39Z</updated>
    - <author>
        <name />
      </author>
    - <content type="application/xml">
      - <m:properties>
          <d:FileName>AirplaneLogo.jpg</d:FileName>
          <d:ServerRelativeUrl>/sites/calcdemo/Lists/Workflow Tests/Attachments/1/AirplaneLogo.jpg</d:Se
        </m:properties>
      </content>
    </entry>
  - <entry>
      <id>http://sp2016/sites/calcdemo/_api/Web/Lists(guid'd87b7f4b-a43c-410a-8a51-3007f42f0465')/I
      <category term="SP.Attachment" scheme="http://schemas.microsoft.com/ado/2007/08/dataservices/sc
```

This workflow is a bit complex due to the setup of the dictionary object and the call to the web services. The basic steps are:

- Create a dictionary variable to hold the list of returned data.
- Build the URL to make the web service call.
- Call the web service.

- Generate the result:
  - ○ A count of attachments, or
  - ○ A list of attachment file names

Steps:

1. This example uses a list with these columns:
   a. **AttachmentCount** (a Number column)
2. See "Common Workflow Steps" for starting a workflow. Select "**SharePoint 2013 Workflow**". (SPD2010 workflows do not have the features we need for this example.)

3. **Add Build Dictionary Action for the header values.**
   This is used to request JSON formatted data instead of XML
   a. Add a **Build Dictionary** action.

   Build this Dictionary (Output to Variable: dictionary)

   b. Click **this** to display the **Build a Dictionary** dialog box.

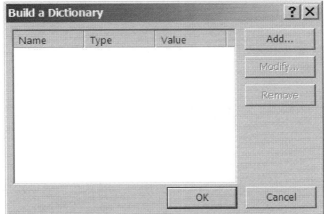

   c. Click **Add**, enter data and click **OK** for each of the following.
   i. Name: **accept**
   ii. Type: **String**
   iii. Value: **application/json; odata=verbose**

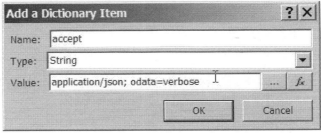

d. Click OK.

e. Click Variable:dictionary.

f. Click Create a new variable.

g. Enter "requestHeaders". (without the quotes)

h. Click OK.

4. Add a Call HTTP Web Service Action.

a. Add a Call HTTP Web Service action.

then Call this HTTP web service with request (ResponseContent to response

|ResponseHeaders to responseHeaders |ResponseStatusCode to Variable: responseCode)

b. Click this.

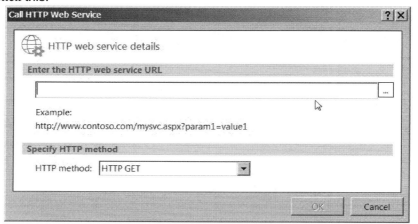

c. Click "..." to display the String Builder dialog box.

d. Click Add or Change Lookup.

e. From Data Source select Workflow Context.

f. From Field from source select Current Site URL. (This will generate a URL to your site. Something like: "https://yourServer/sites/yourSite/yourSubSite/")

g. Click **OK**.

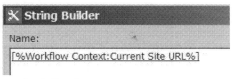

h. Type the following:

_api/web/lists/getbytitle('

i. Click **Add or Change Lookup**.
j. From **Data Source** select **Workflow Context**.
k. From **Field from source** select **List Name**.

l. Click **OK**.

m. Type the following:

')/items(

n. Click **Add or Change Lookup**.
o. From **Data Source** select **Current Item**.

p. From **Field from source** select ID

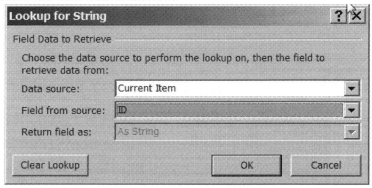

q. Click **OK**.

r. Type the following:

)/AttachmentFiles

s. Verify that the result looks like this:

[%Workflow Context:Current Site URL%]_api/web/lists/getbytitle('
[%Workflow Context:List Name%]')/items([%Current Item:ID%]/
AttachmentFiles

t. Click **OK**.

u. Set the HTTP **method** to: HTTP GET.

v. Click **OK**.

w. Click the dropdown at far right of the **Call HTTP Web Service** action and click
Properties. (You will need to mouse-over the action line to display the dropdown.)

x. Click **RequestHeaders** and select **Variable: requestHeaders** from the dropdown.

y. Click **ResponseContent** and select **Create New Variable** from the dropdown, enter "**responseData**" and click **OK**.

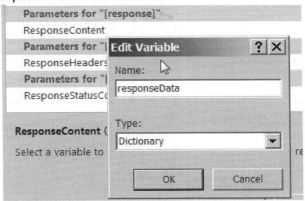

z. click **OK** to close the properties dialog box.

If you run the workflow now, it will get the data, so next we need to decide what to do with it. We will first just count the attachments. The data initially returned is a single JSON object named "d" that contains a single object named "result" that contains the objects (the attachment entries) we need. We will need to extract them from "result".

5. **Extract the attachments data.**

a. Add a **Get an Item from a Dictionary** action.

> then Get <u>item by name or path</u> from <u>dictionary</u> (Output to <u>item</u>)

b. Click **item by name or path**, click "…", enter "**d.result**" and click **OK**.

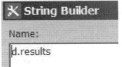

c. Click **dictionary** and select **responseData**.

d. Click **item** and create a new variable named "**attachements**".

> then Get <u>d.results</u> from <u>Variable: responseData</u> (Output to <u>Variable: attachments</u>)

e. Add a **Count Items in a Dictionary** action.

> then Count Items in <u>dictionary</u> (Output to <u>Variable: count2</u>)

f. Click **dictionary** and select **attachments**.

g. Click **Variable: count** and create a new variable named "**FileCount**".

> then Count Items in <u>Variable: attachments</u> (Output to <u>Variable: FileCount</u>)

h. Click **OK**.

i. Now that we have the count, write it to a Number column in your list.

i. Add a **Set Field in Current Item** action.

201

     ii. Click **field** and select your column. ("**AttachmentCount**" for this example.)

     iii. Click **value** and select **FileCount**.

6. Here's the result:

Stage: Stage 1

Build [...] Dictionary (Output to Variable: requestHeaders)

then Call [%Workflow Context:Current Site URL%]... HTTP web service with request (ResponseContent to Variable: responseData |R

then Get d.results from Variable: responseData (Output to Variable: attachments)

then Count Items in Variable: attachments (Output to Variable: FileCount)

then Set AttachmentCount to Variable: FileCount

Transition to stage

Go to End of Workflow

---

7. Add a Calculated Column to your list to display a message about the attached files.

```
=if( ISBLANK([AttachmentCount]),
    "No attachments",
    [AttachmentCount] & " files attached")
```

Title		Attachment Message
Error on sales report	...	2 files attached
Timeout on order entry	...	1 files attached
Incorrect tax amount	...	No attachments

You could also add a workflow loop and extract the file names, which are in the collection we just counted (the "attachments" variable).

12. **Error Messages**

Errors? Who gets errors when writing complicated formulas?

Before chasing an error...

The easiest way to debug the error is to duplicate it in Excel. In Excel you get Intelisense, autocomplete and quick Trial and Error testing. See "The Easiest Way to Write SharePoint Formulas" in Chapter 2.

2	Category	Hardware			
3	Qty	100			
4	Price	650			
5		=IF(Qty < 10, Qty * Price, Qty * Price * 80%)			

The formula contains a syntax error or is not supported

The most common error message for SharePoint formulas is "The formula contains a syntax error or is not supported."

Sorry, something went wrong

The formula contains a syntax error or is not supported.

TECHNICAL DETAILS

GO BACK TO SITE

Common causes:

- Formula is missing a parentheses.   "(" or ")"
- Formula has a misspelled column name.
- A non-supported Excel formula was used. For example: SUBSTITUTE
- You typed a semicolon where a comma was expected, or vice versa. Using a semicolon vs. a comma is a cultural setting in SharePoint. You tried to use the built-in variables [ME]. [TODAY] or [NOW] where they are not supported. (You can use the TODAY() and NOW() functions in Calculated Column formulas, but they are only recalculated when the list item is edited. They are not recalculated on each display of the list.)

Note: Asking your administrator to look up the error in the system logs by using the Correlation ID (GUID) will not help… The error logs only contain the message "The formula contains a syntax error or is not supported".

The formula refers to a column that does not exist.

Common causes:

- Missed-typed column name.
- Square brackets are needed around a column name due to spaces or other special characters.
- You tried to use the built-in variables [ME]. [TODAY] or [NOW] where they are not supported. (You can use the TODAY() and NOW() functions in Calculated Column formulas, but they are only recalculated when the list item is edited. They are not recalculated on each display of the list.)

Sorry, something went wrong

The formula refers to a column that does not exist. Check the formula for spelling mistakes or change the non-existing column to an existing column.

Save Conflict

The "Save Conflict" could mean:

- Another user is making a change to the same column.
- You have the same edit page opened twice.
- You used the back button to get back to the edit screen.

Sorry, something went wrong

Save Conflict
> Your changes conflict with those made concurrently by another user. If you want your changes to be applied, click Back in your Web browser, refresh the page, and resubmit your changes.

Typically solve this by clicking your browser's back button, copy the formula, refresh the page and paste the formula (or repeat the edit).

Calculated columns cannot contain volatile functions like Today and Me

This one is pretty obvious...

- You tried to use the built-in variables [ME]. [TODAY] or [NOW] where they are not supported. (You can use the TODAY() and NOW() functions in Calculated Column formulas, but they are only recalculated when the list item is edited. They are not recalculated on each display of the list.)

Sorry, something went wrong

Calculated columns cannot contain volatile functions like Today and Me.

Errors in the Calculated Result

When the formula is valid, but the data is not as expected, you may see the following error codes in your results.

Tips!

- Most of these errors can be captured by wrapping the formula in an ISERROR test. ISERROR detects these errors: #N/A, #VALUE!, #REF!, #DIV/0!, #NUM!, #NAME?, or #NULL!.
    - #N/A, #REF!, #NAME?, and #NULL! are not typically found in SharePoint formulas.
    - ISERR is the same as ISERROR, except it ignores "#N/A".
    - ISNA checks for "#N/A". (But not too useful in SharePoint as "#N/A" is returned from the VLOOKUP, HLOOKUP, LOOKUP, or MATCH functions, none of which are supported by SharePoint formulas.)
- The ISNUMBER, ISTEXT, ISNONTEXT functions can be used to check for invalid data. When used with an IF function, these can return a nicer error message, or an alternate value.

#VALUE!

- The FIND function did not find a match.
- A formula tried to use text in a math operation. (I.e. a Single Line of Text field was used for numbers and the user typed "na" instead of a 0. "=[SomeColumn] / 2" will then return "#VALUE!".
- The VALUE, CEILING, FLOOR or other math function could not covert the text to a number, date or time.
- The AND or OR function has no Boolean tests. (Example: =AND("abc", "xyz")

#DIV/0!

- The calculation has a divide by zero.

#NUM!

- The DATEDIF function is being used with the second date being smaller than the first date.
- If number and significance parameters have different signs, the CEILING function returns #NUM!.
- The SQRT or other function returned an imaginary number such as SQRT(-2).

If your error message is not listed above:

- Do a general web search for the error message.
- Post your question at:
  - techcommunity.microsoft.com/t5/SharePoint/ct-p/SharePoint
  - sharepoint.stackexchange.com
  - social.technet.microsoft.com/Forums/sharepoint/en-US/home
  - answers.microsoft.com/en-us/msoffice/forum/msoffice_sharepoint

Index

N

O

P

R

S